THE UNIVERSITY OF
WINCHESTER

Armageddon Averted

Armageddon Averted

The Soviet Collapse, 1970–2000

STEPHEN KOTKIN

OXFORD
UNIVERSITY PRESS

OXFORD
UNIVERSITY PRESS

Oxford New York

Auckland Bangkok Buenos Aires Cape Town
Chennai Dar es Salaam Delhi Hong Kong Istanbul
Karachi Kolkata Kuala Lumpur Madrid Melbourne
Mexico City Mumbai Nairobi São Paulo Shanghai
Taipei Tokyo Toronto

© Stephen Kotkin 2001

The moral rights of the author have been asserted

First published by Oxford University Press, Inc., 2001
First published as an Oxford University Press paperback, 2003
198 Madison Avenue, New York, New York 10016

www.oup.com

Oxford is a registered trademark of
Oxford University Press

Library of Congress Cataloging in Publication Data
Kotkin, Stephen.
Armageddon averted : the Soviet collapse, 1970–2000 / Stephen Kotkin.
p. cm.
Includes bibliographical references and index.
ISBN-13 978-0-19-516894-5
ISBN 0-19-280245-3 (cloth)   ISBN 0-19-516894-1 (pbk.)
1. Soviet Union—History—1953–1985.
2. Soviet Union—History—1985–1991.
3. Communism—Soviet Union—History.
I. Title
DK274. K635 2001
947.085 21   12589041

5 7 9 10 8 6

Printed in the United States of America
on acid-free paper

In memory of my great-grandfather

Michael Korolewicz

(1889–1969)

who had been a teacher in tsarist Poland and in America
built a chrome, silver, and gold plating business. He used
to take me to the park, beginning when I was in a stroller,
and talk history.

Preface to the paperback edition

Never will I forget coming back evenings to the Vyborg Hotel in Leningrad, in 1984, and seeing a hat or article of clothing afloat in the nearby Black Gulch (*Chernaia rechka*), indicating that another drunk had fallen in and drowned. Even today, some academics continue to debate whether the Soviet system could reform, but the substantive question was whether it could reform and be stabilized in the face of a capitalist West utterly transformed after World War II. In those specific circumstances, socialist reform (liberalization) entailed collapse. Perversely, it was the Communist fable of a Lenin supposedly gentler than Stalin—the myth of socialism with a human face— that triggered the benign demise of Lenin's police state. The Black Gulch swallowed itself, but it left an immense residue. After 1991, the myths of 'reform' and of Western 'aid' helped deflect a full reckoning with the Communist era.

In the two years since this book was published (three since it was written), Russia has continued to offer encouragement, with undercurrents of disquiet. Besides an appreciable learning curve, the overriding influences on further development (or lack thereof) remain the Soviet inheritance: the oil and resource-dominated economy, the world context, and the growing urge to compete more effectively in it. Russia's strategic setting astride Europe, the Middle East, and the Far East, its U.N. Security Council veto, and Soviet-era doomsday arsenal focus attention. But Russia's long-term prospects will be determined by the vicissitudes of internal transformation, especially of its unreconstructed military-security apparatus, its judiciary, and its regulatory agencies. Even many officials now recognize a need to enhance the conditions for small and medium businesses and average property owners and to reinvest liberally in the country's notable educational system. Pragmatic foreign policy pursuits include closer ties rooted in mutual interest with all neighbors, particularly with Europe but also the United States, belated admission into the World Trade Organization, and some day, a GDP to match Portugal's.

Thanks are due to my new editors at OUP New York, Peter Ginna and Linda Robbins, and to readers and reviewers who pointed out errors, which have been corrected. A chapter prepared for the hardback on the new states besides Russia—excised for space reasons—appeared separately as 'Trashcanistan,' *The New Republic,* 15 April 2002 (www.tnr.com).

Preface

My first encounter with the Soviet bloc took place one summer in 1983. As a graduate student of Habsburg history, I made my way to Prague from northern California to advance my language skills in pursuit of a bygone empire. On the day of my arrival in the capital of Bohemia, I discovered a mass 'socialist peace rally'. Surprised to hear a familiar voice booming over the loudspeakers, I pushed my way through the crowd to the front, and sure enough it was him: the then socialist mayor of Berkeley.

Socialism in the bloc turned out to be nothing like what I, as an American, had been led to believe. Rather than an ironclad dictatorship in a world completely unto itself, or an unremarkable system gradually converging with that of the West, it proved to be very different from the West yet increasingly penetrated by the West, and its highly rigid structures had to be constantly circumvented to make them function. It was full of incessant complaining but also thoroughgoing conformism, and had a relatively impoverished material culture but a richly engaging sociability. I made up my mind that, upon returning to the University of California, I would begin the study of Russian, and switch empires.

These were the days of Polish Solidarity and its underground 'flying universities', which were hailed as 'civil society' triumphant, but one of my professors, a noted Frenchman, spent considerable effort urging me to use caution with the notion of 'civil society', which he called 'the new ideology of the intellectual class'. Another professor, in French history, told me that civil society could not exist without private property. Two very fine professors of Russian history helped me get up to speed on a country I hardly knew. When perestroika suddenly broke in the Soviet Union, which of course did not have institutionalized private property, I was saved from what American intellectuals made their principal (mis)interpretation of Soviet, and then Russian, developments, and instead puzzled over the nature of the state and institutions, as well as Soviet categories of thought.

My first trip to the Soviet Union took place in the summer of 1984, the reign of Chernenko, for a Russian language programme in Leningrad, with side trips to Ukraine and to the site of the Big Three meeting during the Second World War to decide the fate of Europe—Yalta, where I got sick and threw up. In the years following that initial foray, I have been able to undertake very extensive travels, sometimes living for extended periods in the Soviet and the post-Soviet world, doing research in or familiarizing myself with every Soviet republic, except for Turkmenistan, and most countries in Eastern Europe, before and after 1989–91, as well as China and Japan. Mainly, I spent the years of Soviet and then Russian 'reform' researching and writing a two-volume, French-style 'total history' of the past and present of a Soviet steel town.

From that rust-belt vantage point, it could not have been any more obvious that reform was collapse, and that the collapse would not be overcome for quite some time to come.

Convinced well before 1991 that the 'conservatives' were right, that Soviet socialism and the Union were being (inadvertently) destroyed by Gorbachev's perestroika, I had sought an audience and got it with the number two man in the Soviet hierarchy, Yegor Ligachev, in his office at Party HQ on Old Square. To be inside the Central Committee complex, whose history and intrigues I knew from reading, had a surreal quality. Beyond attaining the forbidden, I wanted to figure out why neither Ligachev nor anyone else at the top had tried to remove Gorbachev and undo the reforms. This exchange turned out to be one of several long meetings we ended up having, the rest taking place in the exclusive dacha compound of the top Soviet leadership, others of whom I also met. Here, too, was collapse.

I shall never forget later escorting Ligachev around New York, demonstrating and explaining the vast universe of private small businesses and immigrant-run eateries for hours on end, only to have him ask over and over again who in the government was responsible for feeding the huge urban population. The world was as lucky in the pathetic, principled Ligachev as it was in the masterly, principled Gorbachev. Evicted, their place was taken by morally less promising people, who fought violently over the massive spoils of Communist-era offices, state dachas, apartment complexes, and vacation resorts. Making the rounds, I began to see that the best way to understand Russian politics was mostly to ignore the grand 'reform' programmes, which would soon be added to their predecessors already choking the archives, and instead closely to track prime real estate.

Before 1991, I had made a point of inspecting the premises of the once almighty State Planning Commission (Gosplan) and State Supply Commission (Gossnab), which together had planned an economy over one-sixth of the earth. After 1991, I would go back, to see the new (and old), or reshuffled, inhabitants. In the chaos of perestroika, I also gained easy access to party headquarters in the republic capitals and many provinces; after these edifices had been renamed, I went back to find many of the people I had known, usually with higher positions, though not a few had moved laterally, and the provincials had often been elevated to the capital. And so it emerged that, just as social constituencies, whether in the rust belt or state bureaucracy, provided the keys to understanding the inherent limits to any proposed political programme, patterns of sociability afforded the keys to grasping the dynamics of power.

Friends I had made while an exchange student at Moscow State University in the 1980s were, by the 1990s, in the Russian government or Kremlin, and the chance to share in their life trajectories and perspectives has been extremely illuminating. Lower down the social hierarchy, in 2000–1, I was equally privileged to carry out an eight-month investigation of an ambitious volunteer initiative called the Civic Education Project. In fifteen countries, from Hungary to Kazakhstan, Estonia to Azerbaijan, my task, as a consultant for the Open Society Institute, entailed interviewing scores of university administrators, hundreds of academics, and thousands of students. It was, with a few exceptions, a grim inventory of a world, ten years after the Soviet collapse, still undergoing deep political and economic involution. But everywhere the university students proved to be a remarkable lot, multi-talented and auspiciously responsive to educational opportunities.

Some of the material in this book first appeared in the *New Republic,* and I am extremely grateful to Leon Wieseltier for that opportunity. For similar reasons I would also like to thank the *East European Constitutional Review* and its editor, Stephen Holmes. Catherine Clarke of Oxford University Press commissioned the book and with Catherine Humphries and Hilary Walford guided it to completion. Tyler Felgenhauer compiled the index. Leonard Benardo, Laura Engelstein, Geoffrey Hosking, Sara Mosle, Philip Nord, Steven Solnick, Amir Weiner, and William Wohlforth offered incisive commentary on drafts of the text. Special thanks also to Princeton University's Liechtenstein Institute on Self-Determination, directed by Wolfgang Danspeckgruber, and to the National Council for East European and Eurasian Research in Washington, DC, for support of research and writing. I love my wife, Soyoung Lee, so much I can barely say.

Contents

Note on the text

All translations from Russian sources are the author's. For transliteration of personal and place names, whether in the text or in discursive endnotes, common usage has been preferred (Yeltsin rather than El'tsin). But for authors' names and the titles of Russian-language books and articles in the endnotes, the US Library of Congress system has been adopted (Evgenii rather than Yevgeny).

List of plates

Whilst every effort has been made to secure permissions, we may have failed in a few cases to trace the copyright holders. We apologize for any apparent negligence.

List of maps

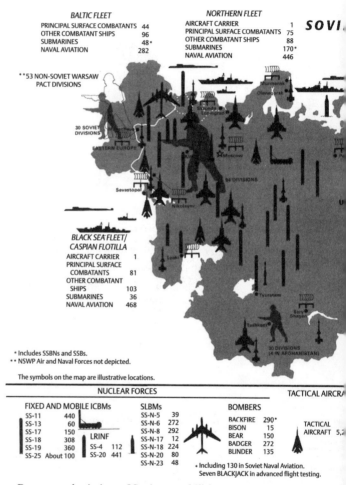

BALTIC FLEET

PRINCIPAL SURFACE COMBATANTS	44
OTHER COMBATANT SHIPS	96
SUBMARINES	48*
NAVAL AVIATION	282

NORTHERN FLEET

AIRCRAFT CARRIER	1
PRINCIPAL SURFACE COMBATANTS	75
OTHER COMBATANT SHIPS	88
SUBMARINES	170*
NAVAL AVIATION	446

SOVI

**53 NON-SOVIET WARSAW PACT DIVISIONS

30 SOVIET DIVISIONS

EASTERN EUROPE

Murmansk
Olenegorsk

Severo
Leningrad

Moscow

Sevastopol

Nikolayev

Lyak

50 DIVISIONS

Tyuratam

Sary
Shagan

Tashkent

30 DIVISIONS
(4 IN AFGHANISTAN)

**BLACK SEA FLEET/
CASPIAN FLOTILLA**

AIRCRAFT CARRIER	1
PRINCIPAL SURFACE COMBATANTS	81
OTHER COMBATANT SHIPS	103
SUBMARINES	36
NAVAL AVIATION	468

* Includes SSBNs and SSBs.
** NSWP Air and Naval Forces not depicted.

The symbols on the map are illustrative locations.

NUCLEAR FORCES

FIXED AND MOBILE ICBMs

SS-11	440
SS-13	60
SS-17	150
SS-18	308
SS-19	360
SS-25	About 100

LRINF

SS-4	112
SS-20	441

SLBMs

SS-N-5	39
SS-N-6	272
SS-N-8	292
SS-N-17	12
SS-N-18	224
SS-N-20	80
SS-N-23	48

BOMBERS

BACKFIRE	290*
BISON	15
BEAR	150
BADGER	272
BLINDER	135

* Including 130 in Soviet Naval Aviation.
Seven BLACKJACK in advanced flight testing.

TACTICAL AIRCR

TACTICAL AIRCRAFT	5,2

1 Pentagon depiction of Soviet capabilities

Petropavlovsk

Krasnoyarsk

Komsomol'sk

57 DIVISIONS
(8 IN MONGOLIA)

Mihalenko

Vladivostok

PACIFIC OCEAN FLEET

AIRCRAFT CARRIERS	2
PRINCIPAL SURFACE COMBATANTS	84
OTHER COMBATANT SHIPS	121
SUBMARINES	120
NAVAL AVIATION	560

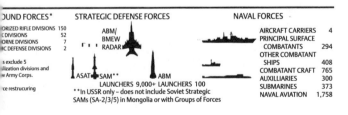

OUND FORCES *

ORIZED RIFLE DIVISIONS	150
DIVISIONS	52
ORNE DIVISIONS	7
IC DEFENSE DIVISIONS	2

s exclude 5
ilization divisions and
Army Corps.

ce restrucuring

STRATEGIC DEFENSE FORCES

ABM/
BMEW
RADAR

ASAT SAM **   ABM
LAUNCHERS 9,000+ LAUNCHERS 100
** In USSR only – does not include Soviet Strategic
SAMs (SA-2/3/5) in Mongolia or with Groups of Forces

NAVAL FORCES

AIRCRAFT CARRIERS	4
PRINCIPAL SURFACE COMBATANTS	294
OTHER COMBATANT SHIPS	408
COMBATANT CRAFT	765
AUXILLIARIES	300
SUBMARINES	373
NAVAL AVIATION	1,758

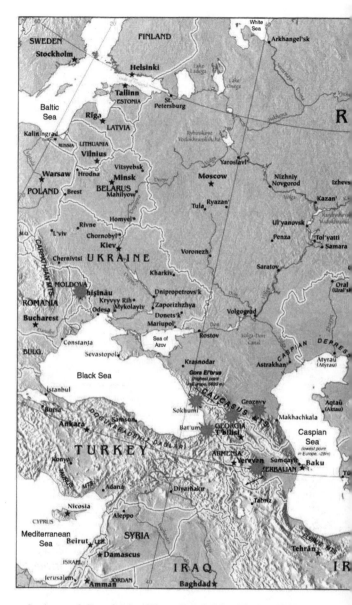

2 Soviet and Post-Soviet Wars: Karabakh, Ajaria, Abkhazia, Osse
Ingushetia, Chechnhya (all in the Caucasus); Moldova (betw
Romania and Ukraine); Tajikistan (bordering Afghanistan).

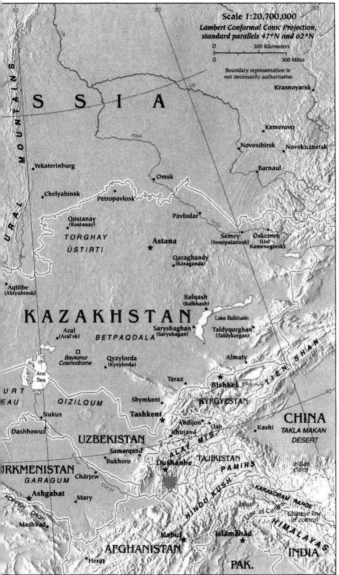

Introduction

Reviewing the history of international relations in the modern era, which might be considered to extend from the middle of the seventeenth century to the present, I find it hard to think of any event more strange and startling, and at first glance more inexplicable, than the sudden and total disintegration and disappearance from the international scene ... of the great power known successively as the Russian Empire and then the Soviet Union.

(George F. Kennan, 1995)

The problems that the Soviet leaders have to solve simply have no solutions ... However, the Soviet leaders are not going to commit political suicide.

(Vladimir Bukovsky, 1989)

Virtually everyone seems to think the Soviet Union was collapsing before 1985. They are wrong. Most people also think the Soviet collapse ended in 1991. Wrong again. These points become readily apparent when one examines the period 1970–2000 as an integrated whole, tracing the arc of Soviet economic and political institutions before and after 1991, and when one combines a view from deep inside the system with a sober sense of the precise role of the wider context. Forget about the dominant tropes of 'neo-liberal reforms' and 'Western aid' for describing post-Soviet Russia, let alone 'emerging civil society' for characterizing the late Soviet period. What happened in the Soviet Union, and continued in Russia, was the sudden onset, and then inescapable prolongation, of the death agony of an entire world comprising non-market economics and anti-liberal institutions.

The monumental second world collapse, in the face of a more powerful first world wielding the market and liberal institutions, was triggered not by military pressure but by Communist ideology. The KGB and to a lesser extent the CIA secretly reported that, beginning in the 1970s, the Soviet Union was overcome by malaise. But even though Soviet socialism had clearly lost the competition with the West, it was lethargically stable, and could have continued muddling on for quite some time. Or, it might have tried a Realpolitik retrenchment, cutting back on superpower ambitions, legalizing and then institutionalizing market economics to revive its fortunes, and holding tightly to central power by using political repression. Instead, the Soviet Union embarked on a quest to realize the dream of 'socialism with a human face'.

This humanist vision of reform emerged in the post-Stalin years, under Nikita Khrushchev, and it stamped an entire generation—a generation, led by Mikhail Gorbachev, that lamented the crushing of the 1968 Prague Spring, and that came to power in Moscow in 1985. They believed the planned economy could be reformed essentially without introducing full private property or market prices. They believed relaxing censorship would increase the population's allegiance to socialism. They believed the Communist Party could be democratized. They were mistaken. Perestroika, unintentionally, destroyed the planned economy, the allegiance to Soviet socialism, and, in the end, the party, too. And the blow to the party unhinged the Union, which the party alone had held together.

That the man at the pinnacle of power in Moscow—a committed, true-believing Communist Party General Secretary—was engaged in a virtuoso, yet inadvertent liquidation of the Soviet system, made for high drama, which few appreciated for what it was. When crowds suddenly cracked the Berlin Wall in late 1989, and when Eastern Europe was allowed to break from the Soviet grip, dumbfounded analysts (myself included) began to wonder if the rest of the Kremlin's empire, the Union republics, might also separate. That made the years 1990–1 a time of high drama, because, although it had been destabilized by romantic idealism, the Soviet system still commanded a larger and more powerful military and repressive apparatus than any state in history. It had more than enough nuclear weapons to destroy or blackmail the world, and a vast storehouse of chemical and biological weapons, with all requisite delivery systems. The Soviet Union also had more than five million soldiers, deployed from Budapest to Vladivostok, and hundreds of thousands more troops in KGB and interior ministry battalions. It experienced almost no major mutinies in any of these forces. And yet, they were never fully used—not to save a collapsing empire, nor even to wreak havoc out of spite.

Of course, the Soviet break-up was accompanied by more than half a dozen civil wars—in Chechnya, Karabakh, Ingushetia, Ossetia, Abkhazia, Adjaria (all in the Causcasus), Moldova (another mal-intentioned Stalin contrivance), and Tajikistan (bordering Afghanistan). These conflicts resulted in many thousands of deaths, several million refugees, and a number of internationally unrecognized statelets that *de facto* subdivided the fifteen successor states. Even Ukraine, which avoided a civil war, had in its far west a tiny self-declared 'republic' of Sub-Carpathian Rus. But bear in mind that Ukraine's Russian population, at more than eleven million (20 per cent), constituted the largest ethnic minority in Europe. Kazakhstan had another five million Russians (about 33 per cent of its population). Overall, with seventy-one million former Soviet inhabitants (one of every four) suddenly living outside their nominal national homeland, if they had a national homeland at all, and with the horrid example of much smaller Yugoslavia's catastrophic break-up right next door, one shudders to think of the manipulative wars, indeed the nuclear, chemical, or biological Armageddon, that *could have* accompanied the Soviet collapse.

Who had anticipated that the Soviet Union would meekly dissolve itself? Those few analysts who did perceive the depth of Soviet problems, and the structural impediments to solving them, never imagined that such a police state would just let go, quietly. Of the twenty million members of the former USSR Communist Party, perhaps two to three million made up the higher elite—a formidable bastion of power that encompassed the party apparatus, state bureaucracy, military, and KGB. Even if suspicions abounded that many of these officials had become cynical about the official ideology, analysts remained convinced that collectively they would *never* permit the overthrow of the system, if only to protect their own interests. Thus, notwithstanding the profusion of autopsies on the Soviet collapse, a major riddle persists: beyond Gorbachev, why did the immense Soviet elite, armed to the teeth with loyal internal forces and weapons, fail to defend either socialism or the Union with all its might?

This riddle becomes even more challenging when we note that once the dangers of dissolution had become evident to the whole world, elements of the most privileged groups in the USSR gave the shaken edifice a final shove over the edge. Could the elite of a great power really have permitted and then *facilitated* its country's dissolution *without* having suffered foreign occupation, insubordination among its massive military and police, or even sustained civil disobedience? Indeed it could. One of my main tasks in this short volume is to elucidate how and why the Soviet elite destroyed its own system, keeping in mind that the greatest surprise of the Soviet collapse was not that it happened—though that was shocking enough—but the absence of an all-consuming conflagration.

Now that it is gone, the Soviet Union has revealed itself—for those who still did not know—to have been much more than a dictatorship and military behemoth. It was also a comprehensive experiment in non-capitalist modernity or socialism, and an improbable revival and transformation of the tsarist empire into a quasi-federation of states. The largest of those internal non-capitalist Soviet states was the Russian republic. A product of the Soviet Union, Russia inherited everything that had caused the Soviet collapse, as well as the collapse itself. In the 1990s, the collapse was still called 'reform' (albeit 'radical'), but the public battles for and against reform were accompanied by both continuation of the collapse and tectonic processes of institutional recombination. Herein lies another of the main tasks of this book: elucidating the importance for Russia of the Soviet inheritance.

Beyond the myriad surviving agencies and ministries—such as the State Procuracy and the KGB—one could see in newly founded institutions remnants of the Soviet era, from the Central Committee apparat (Presidential Administration) to the State Planning Commission (Economics Ministry). Indeed, all Soviet-era office buildings were still standing, and in some cases they were enlarged, to accommodate both former and additional cadres. The 'new' people were not, of course, from Mars, but from elite Soviet schools and the Communist Youth League, members of the second and third echelons who rose more quickly in the chaos of dissolution, and who combined a mixture of new and old. In addition, the entire non-market Soviet economy, ten time zones of antiquated heavy industry and decaying infrastructure, was also still in place, providing the bedrock of communities as well as of social constituencies. These were the political and economic structures that had caused the Soviet Union to fall further and further behind the West starting in the 1970s, and they served as the building blocks of the new Russia, which fell even further behind.

The idea that the collapse suddenly ended in December 1991, and that a handful of new 'democrats' or 'radical reformers' had come to power, was silly. Yet, to most analysts, it proved irresistible, whether they cheered or jeered Russia's 'transition'. What seemed to matter was not the make-up of society and the economy, or the working of state institutions, but only solemn pronouncements of intent and streams of presidential decrees, most of which went unimplemented. In the United States during the same decade, commentators properly scoffed at President Bill Clinton's plan to overhaul the US health-care system. Remake one-seventh of the US economy, against a vast array of entrenched, powerful interest groups! Yet many of these same people assumed that Russia's ability to transform its *entire economy and social structure*—seven-sevenths—was merely a matter of 'will power' on the part of 'reformers' or even of a single man. Technocratic 'reform' *in some other country* is the opiate of experts and pundits. Give any country some 15,000 rust-belt factories, perhaps two-thirds of them non-viable in market conditions, as well as several million brigands empowered to act in the name of state, and see how quickly such a place achieves the 'transition' to paradise.

Predictably, expectations of an immediate, total transformation gave way to profound disillusionment, and an equally off-the-mark, and similarly widely shared view that Russia was a unique, reformer-induced disaster. As of 2001, amid the ongoing and immense Soviet collapse, Russia was indeed a mess. But it was also a stable mess, and, although written off, it was finally groping towards the very institutional reforms that people erroneously thought were taking place during the 1990s.

Too often Russia has been judged far more harshly than, or without reference to, the rest of the former Soviet Union, despite the fact that on most political and economic indicators Russia compared favourably with every former Soviet republic except tiny Estonia. And, stuck as it was in a multigenerational slog to institutionalize a market economy, and maybe also something resembling a Russian version of a liberal polity, it had already mastered many of the distinguishing attributes of another very large country that used to be its main rival: gross income disparities, contempt for the public interest, mass corporate tax evasion, pervasive recourse to political power in the market place, hyper-commercialized media, money-besotted elections, and demagogy.

The following overview of the last two decades of the Soviet Union and the first decade of post-Soviet Russia is organized partly chronologically, and partly analytically. It does not focus on supposed cultural proclivities or deficiencies, imagined nationalism, evil oligarchs, or Western advice, whose significance (good and bad) has been grossly inflated. Rather, the analysis focuses on elites, and proceeds in terms of structural considerations: a Communist Party generation, led by Mikhail Gorbachev, profoundly shaped by socialist idealism, which emerged to the fore when the previous leadership finally died off; the world view and hopes of 285 million people living within the socialist ideological space; the planned economy and its cost-unconscious, oppressively heavy-industrial physical plant; and, especially, the institutional dynamics of the Soviet state and of the Russian state. Since there is no history without contingency, the narrative also spotlights the attempts to articulate and implement policies, and their unexpected consequences. Ultimately, though, the Soviet collapse and post-Soviet Russia's contradictory first decade would remain inexplicable except as part of broad changes in the world during and after the Second World War. Mine is therefore both a historical and a geopolitical analysis.

1

History's cruel tricks

Then Leonid Ilich [Brezhnev] appeared . . . We lived
fabulously, quietly stealing, quietly drinking.
[A voice interjects: not quietly.]
So be it.

(Ion Druţă, Moldavian writer)

Plant closure has become a depressingly common-
place feature of industrial life. . . . Millions of people
. . . have experienced directly or indirectly the consequences of closure upon their own lives or upon
those of their friends, relatives or communities.

(Tony Dickson and David Judge, on the capitalist
world in the Brezhnev era)

Between 1970 and 1973, the world market price for crude
oil moved steadily upwards. A nearly two-decade run
ended during which supply had outpaced demand. More
than that, spare capacity had disappeared, meaning that
limited cutbacks in production could expect to have dramatic effects on price. When, in October 1973, the Arabs

and Israelis suddenly went to war for the fourth time, Arab states, including the previously reluctant Saudis, announced a decision to roll out the 'oil weapon'. After so many years, such talk had come to seem like crying wolf. This time, however, the Arab nations made good the threat. And, whereas the Middle East war concluded as abruptly as it had started, when Egypt agreed to a ceasefire in late October, the coordinated cutbacks in oil output took on a life of their own. Arcane oil jargon— 'differentials', 'inventory build'—spread into water-cooler conversations and White House policy sessions.[1] Public relations firms spun stories to show why big oil companies were not at all to blame. Government and industry belatedly initiated campaigns to encourage energy conservation among consumers who only the day before had been being goaded to indulge. But probably the most absurd moment of the 'oil shock' involved stepped-up exhortations for America to switch from energy-intensive industries to what were called knowledge-intensive industries, as if the US economy were governed by Soviet-style planners, and not the market.

Oil prices rocketed up 400 per cent in 1973, in just a few months, and the car industry, whose products were defiantly large and gas guzzling, suffered a crushing blow. Also clobbered were broad sectors tied to cars, such as steel manufacture. Of course, before 1973, many giant, energy-intensive 'Fordist' factories, producing big batches of capital goods, had experienced competitive troubles. But for those that had been muddling through, the oil crisis brought an inescapable day of reckoning. Between 1973 and 1975, US GDP dropped 6 per cent, while unemployment doubled to 9 per cent. Western Europe, which was far more dependent on oil from the Persian Gulf, suffered proportionately. Japan, probably the country most dependent on Middle East oil, saw its GDP drop for the first time in the post-war period. Beyond the immediate downturn, the entire fossil-fuel industrial economy—which had arisen in the late nineteenth century and which in the first half of the twentieth century had adopted mass production—seemed to be heading towards extinction.

In 1970s England, Sheffield and its surrounding industrial zone lost more than 150,000 jobs in steel; many more jobs vanished in engineering industries, and the city council became Sheffield's largest employer.[2] During the same decade, Germany's powerhouse Ruhr Valley and its multitude of steelworks shed 100,000 jobs. In Pennsylvania—which had once been championed as the 'Ruhr Valley of America'—'Black Friday' (30 September 1977) delivered a body blow to Bethlehem, whose steel had gone into the George Washington Bridge connecting Manhattan and New Jersey, the Golden Gate Bridge across San Francisco Bay, the National Gallery of Art in Washington, DC, and many of the silos for Intercontinental Ballistic Missiles. The US's entire industrial heartland of the eight Great Lake states—Ohio, Michigan, Illinois, Indiana, Wisconsin, Minnesota, New York, as well as Pennsylvania—was devastated.

More than 1,000 factories closed in the US over the 1970s.[3] In a howl of desperation, two authors wrote that 'we are currently witnessing the decline of industrial America, the bankruptcy or deterioration of some once-mighty manufacturing enterprises'.[4] Other commentators more accurately noted the end not of industry *per se*, but a wrenching changeover to what was called flexible manu-facturing.[5] Yet, although manufacturing in the American Midwest began to grow again in the mid-1980s, manu-facturing employment failed to recover at the same rate. In a few instances, even Big Steel pulled itself out of a hole, but the communities stayed down. 'The Gary Works repre-sents one of the most impressive turnarounds in the his-tory of US industry,' a steel industry analyst told a reporter in 1988. But, after a reinvestment of $2.9 billion over seven years, the restructured factory complex, which had once employed 21,000 people, had just 7,500 employees, with further reductions anticipated. 'It's a great success story for the company,' Gary's mayor told a reporter, 'but it has been a painful experience for us'.[6]

This wrenching of industries and communities left an indelible mark on the culture and popular psyche. A cheeky British film entitled *The Full Monty* (1997) retro-spectively spotlighted a group of down-and-out steel-workers who hit upon a survival scheme: organize their own potbellied male striptease, recruiting performers from an unemployment queue. The film was set in Sheffield, and opened with footage from a bygone civic-booster film about a 'city on the move, the jewel in

Yorkshire's crown'. Now, its idle men were compelled to show their jewels to get by. The film's soundtrack appropriately featured disco, as in the industrial classic, *Saturday Night Fever* (1979), about a blue-collar dancing king, which had helped set off the late 1970s disco craze with the anthem of irrepressible dreams, 'Staying Alive'. Desperate times brought desperate approaches. In Johnstown, Pennsylvania, 'tour buses idle outside the moldering steel mills', wrote a *New York Times Magazine* reporter in 1996. He described how Johnstown was 'heading into a future in which the economy will be fed by an ambitious, seemingly quixotic experiment called heritage tourism', which 'retails the often unhappy narratives of unlucky places, and is clearly a growth industry'.[7]

Monuments to misfortune soon pockmarked the entire industrial landscape of the West. The increases in oil prices in the 1970s had crystallized larger trends. Henry Kissinger, who served as President Richard Nixon's Secretary of State during what Washington took to calling the Arab oil embargo, later wrote that it 'altered irrevocably the world as it had grown up in the post-war period'.[8] Kissinger had in mind the geopolitical balance of power and the new centrality of international economics that complicated diplomacy. So-called stagflation—high unemployment (stagnation) plus inflation—confounded America's leading economists, and Watergate paralysed and disgraced Washington. Saigon and South Vietnam fell to the Communists in 1975. With much of US industry undergoing a painful overhaul, the superpower appeared at a low point, not at a crossroads leading to a resounding triumph in the cold war.

Oil windfall and institutional shortfall

From 1910 to 1950, when world oil output rose twelvefold, Russian production rose only fourfold. One expert, writing in the early 1950s, warned that the oil supply is 'the Achilles' heel of the Soviet economy'. After the 1953 CIA-backed coup in Iran had helped block Soviet access to Iranian oil, the extensive Soviet manufacturing economy appeared to be in a pickle. But in 1959—some thirty years after a Soviet scientist had forecast the presence of vast oil deposits in the forested swamps of West Siberia—a gusher was struck. Between 1961 and 1969, five dozen new oilfields were identified, and the Kremlin went from being a net importer of oil to an exporter.[9] Even more fortuitously, this desperately needed Siberian oil rush broke just as the 1973 Arab–Israeli War and accompanying oil shock caused an unexpected leap in world oil prices, and the greatest economic boon the Soviet Union ever experienced. Without the discovery of Siberian oil, the Soviet Union might have collapsed decades earlier.

From 1973 to 1985, energy exports accounted for 80 per cent of the USSR's expanding hard currency earnings. And that was not all. Other oil exporting countries—top customers for Soviet weapons—saw their oil revenues increase from $23 billion in 1972 to $140 billion in 1977.

Many Arab oil states went on military spending sprees, increasing Moscow's oil windfall. What to do with all that cash? The Soviet leadership used its oil revenues to cushion the impact of the oil shock on its East European satellites. Oil money also paid for a huge Soviet military build-up that, incredibly, enabled the country to reach rough parity with the US. And it helped defray the costs of the war in Afghanistan, launched in the late 1970s. Oil money also went into higher salaries and better perks for the ever-expanding Soviet elite. And oil financed the acquisition of Western technology for making cars, synthetic fibres, and other products for consumers, as well as Western feed for Soviet livestock. In future, the inhabitants of the Soviet Union would look back fondly on the Brezhnev era, recalling the cornucopia of sausages that had been available in state stores at subsidized prices.

Oil seemed to save the Soviet Union in the 1970s, but it merely delayed the inevitable. The USSR had risen to become the world's largest producer of oil and natural gas, and the third largest of coal, but it nonetheless suffered chronic energy shortages—what the leading expert aptly called 'a crisis amid plenty'. That was because Soviet factories consumed energy in horribly gluttonous quantities, as if it were free. Then, in 1983, Siberian oil output began to decline. Output would recover in 1986, but after that it again declined, this time uninterruptedly. Making matters worse, in 1986 world oil prices plummeted by 69 per cent, to one of their lowest levels in the post-war period. And the dollar, the currency of the oil trade, also dropped like a stone. 'Overnight,' the expert wrote, 'the windfall oil and dollar profits the Soviets had been enjoying for years were wiped out'.[10] By this time, hungover from its long oil bender, the Soviet leadership was belatedly trying to address its profound structural economic troubles.

Those troubles derived from the country's successes. Whereas, in the 1920s, the Soviet economy had been about 20 per cent industry, transport, and construction, by the mid-1980s that percentage had risen to around 70. No other country ever had such a high percentage of its economy in big factories and mines. And much of Soviet industry had been built during the 1930s, or rebuilt after the destruction of the Second World War according to 1930s specifications. The USSR's Bethlehem Pennsylvanias and Sheffields numbered *in the thousands*, and they were even more antiquated. But, flush with its oil windfall, the Soviet Union had avoided the painful devastation that befell the substantial, yet smaller, rust belts of the United States, Great Britain, and Germany. But it could not do so forever. In the 1990s, the overthrow of socialist planning would lay bare a far greater challenge of massive enterprise restructuring. Post-Communist Russia would inherit, and grandly privatize, history's largest ever assemblage of obsolete equipment.

Socialism's politically driven economy proved very good—too good—at putting up a rust belt; and, unlike a market economy, socialism proved very bad at taking its rust belt down. What had once been a source of the Soviet

Union's strength and legitimization would become, when Russia rejoined the world economy, an enormous energy-consuming, value-subtracting burden, and ultimately, an invitation to scavenge and plunder. In the 1990s, export earnings from energy sources would continue—extending the elite's post-1973 oil debauch. Rather than supporting a huge military build-up and a sprawling empire, however, the oil (and gas) money would go into private offshore bank accounts and hideaways on the Spanish and French Rivieras. Russia's economic debacle embodied a delayed end, on a bigger scale and slightly camouflaged by oil flows, to an entire industrial epoch, of which it, too, formed a part, and whose demise had been clearly visible twenty years before in Germany's Ruhr Valley, Sheffield and England's North, and America's Midwest.

And that was just half the story. Obsolete industry can in theory be overcome, no matter how vast its extent. But even after junking planning, Russia was not able to overcome its unprecedentedly large industrial junk heap, or quickly to create substantial new, dynamic sectors. That was because Russia lacked the indispensable liberal institutions that make markets work, while it possessed a plethora of the kinds of institutions that inhibit effective market operation. Here was a banal but useful reminder: the market is not an economic but a political and institutional phenomenon. The proof of that proposition lies not in countries such as the United States, where effective courts and indispensable government regulation are taken for granted, or even ideologically denounced, but in the post-Soviet countries, where most market-facilitating institutions are lacking or function egregiously. Thus, obsolete as its physical plant had become, the Soviet Union's central dilemma—as post-Soviet Russia would demonstrate—was really political and institutional.

The twentieth century's great turn

The central Soviet dilemma was also geopolitical. In the 1980s the economy of India was arguably in worse shape (for different reasons), but India was not locked in a global superpower competition with the United States (allied with West Germany, France, Britain, Italy, Canada, and Japan). That rivalry, moreover, was not merely economic, technological, and military, but also political, cultural, and moral. From its inception, the Soviet Union had claimed to be an experiment in socialism, a superior alternative to capitalism, for the entire world. If socialism was not superior to capitalism, its existence could not be justified. In the inter-war period, during Stalin's violent crusade to build socialism, capitalism had seemed for many people to be synonymous with world imperialism, the senseless slaughter of the First World War, goose-stepping militarism, and Great Depression unemployment. Against that background, the idea of a non-capitalist world—with the same modern machines but supposedly with social justice—held wide appeal.

But in the Second World War fascism was defeated, and

after the war the capitalist dictatorships embraced democracy. Instead of a final economic crisis anticipated by Stalin and others, capitalism experienced an unprecedented boom, which made the Depression a memory and homeownership a mass phenomenon. Economic growth in the US, after a robust 1950s, hit a phenomenal 52.8 per cent in the 1960s; more significantly, median family income rose 39.7 per cent over the decade. In Japan and West Germany, losers in the Second World War, economic 'miracles' led to revolutions in mass consumption. New media technologies, such as cinema and radio, which had seemed so convenient for interwar dictatorships seeking to spread propaganda, turned out to be conduits of a commercial mass culture impervious to state borders. Finally, all leading capitalist countries embraced the 'welfare state'—a term coined during the Second World War—stabilizing their social orders, and challenging socialism on its own turf. In short, between the 1930s and the 1960s, the image and reality of capitalism changed radically. Affordable Levittown homes, ubiquitous department stores overflowing with inexpensive consumer goods, expanded health and retirement benefits, and increasingly democratic institutions were weapons altogether different from Nazi tanks.

As if that was not pressure enough, the Second World War and its aftermath also set in motion a wave of decolonization, which the Soviet Union sought to exploit but which ended up further undermining its position. The Soviet Union was a land empire, with a twist. Whereas the pre-revolutionary Russian empire comprised only non-ethnic provinces, aside from the Duchy of Finland and the small Central Asian 'protectorates' of Bukhara and Khiva, the Soviet Union consisted of fifteen nationally designated republics with state borders. Beginning in the 1920s, Moscow presided over an expansion of the republics' national institutions and national consciousness, which endured the purges, mass deportations, and Russification. Two of the Union republics, Ukraine and Belarussia, got their own UN seats, and all underwent economic development. Proudly, the Soviet Union contrasted itself with the capitalist empires of Britain or France. By the 1970s, however, after almost all overseas territories controlled by capitalist countries had gained independence, the idea of a better form of empire became an anachronism. The Soviet Union, moreover, did not have just an 'inner empire' but also what George Orwell called an 'outer empire'.

Chasing Hitler out of the Soviet Union back to Berlin presented Stalin with the irresistible opportunity of regaining some tsarist territories not reconquered in 1917–21, and with swallowing much of Eastern Europe. Not content merely to exercise political and military domination, the Soviet Union attempted after 1948 to clone satellite regimes. Yet Sovietization of Eastern Europe took place not during the 1930s Great Depression and fascist militarism, but during the post-war capitalist boom and deployment of comprehensive welfare states. In these altered circumstances, the fate of Soviet socialism was now irrevocably tied to the fate of the regimes in Eastern

Europe. Already in the early 1950s, and especially after Nikita Khrushchev had denounced Stalin in 1956 and Poland and Hungary had erupted in revolt, Eastern Europe weighed down the Soviet leadership. 'If we depart Hungary,' Khrushchev told his colleagues behind closed doors, 'it will give a great boost to the Americans, English, French—the imperialists. They will perceive it as a weakness on our part and go on the offensive'.[11] Despite the crackdown, Hungary was eventually allowed to legalize some private enterprise, while Poland halted the collectivization of agriculture and conceded a prominent role for the Catholic Church, opening fissures in the Soviet model of socialism.

In 1968, Moscow again felt compelled to invade an ostensible ally, to crush the efforts to 'reform' socialism in Czechoslovakia, which became particularly embittered and damaged the USSR's international prestige. Two years later, and again in 1976, mass strikes rocked Poland. In 1978, the first non-Italian since 1523, Karol Woityla, archbishop of Krakow, was chosen pope. The next year, on his first pilgrimage home, more than ten million Poles attended outdoor celebrations of the mass, often weeping with joy. In 1980, Polish workers, inspired by the pope and provoked by price increases, rose en masse, forming a countrywide independent trade union and bringing the socialist system to the point of liquidation. A crackdown by Polish leaders in December 1981 saved the regime, for the time being. To pacify workers the Polish regime had been borrowing from the West to import consumer goods, a dependency that became common across the Soviet bloc. East Germany, which abutted a far richer West Germany, eventually accumulated a $26.5 billion foreign debt, whose servicing absorbed 60 per cent of annual export earnings. But to buy off its walled-in people, the party leadership saw no alternative to increasing consumer imports and thus Western dependence.[12]

In Hungary, Poland, East Germany, and Czechoslovakia, the only force holding back the long-term tidal pull of the West appeared to be Soviet resolve. The acquisition of an outer empire in Eastern Europe—what, again, looked like a Soviet strength—had proved to be a dangerous vulnerability. Of course, in the late 1940s, when Soviet-style socialism first spread to Eastern Europe, it had seemed the leading edge of a possible world takeover, especially after the 1949 victory of the Chinese Communists in the world's most populous country. Few people understood that a major shift had indeed occurred—but in the opposite direction, to the grave detriment of Soviet socialism. Simply put, socialism was utterly dependent on the fortunes of capitalism, and the differences between capitalism in the Great Depression and capitalism in the post-war world were nothing short of earth shattering. No less momentous, the United States, which during the period of the Soviet Union's rise prior to the Second World War had remained somewhat aloof from European and Asian affairs, now assumed a vigorous role as 'leader of the free world', uniting previously fractious capitalist powers under its leadership to counter the Soviet threat.

Imagine a geopolitical contest in which one side says, I will take West Germany and France, you get East Germany and Romania; I will take Britain and Italy, you get Bulgaria and Hungary; I will take Japan and Saudi Arabia, you get Cuba and Angola. Even Communist China became a threat to the Soviet Union after the Chinese split with Moscow and put themselves forward as an alternative model for the Third World. And what a burden Third World entanglements could be! In the 1970s Somalia–Ethiopia conflict, the Soviet Union decided to airlift heavy tanks to Ethiopia, but because long-distance supply planes could carry only a single tank, transport exceeded the cost of the expensive tanks by five times—never mind what a superpower was doing seeking influence chiefly in countries whose main industry was civil war. The US, which had its own ambitions, opposed Soviet influence by arming proxies. And in the 1975 Helsinki Accords, the US exchanged formal recognition of post-war European borders, a long-held dream of the Soviet leadership, for the Soviets' written pledge to uphold human rights. This trade-off, whose importance the CIA completely missed, led to an international legal and moral 'full court press' that Soviet diplomats and negotiators felt alongside Western military, economic, and cultural might.[13]

Panic, humiliation, defection

Leonid Brezhnev, meeting with President Richard Nixon at San Clemente, California, in June 1973, had made a desperate attempt to protect Soviet–American détente by urging a new joint initiative for the Middle East. But Henry Kissinger dismissed Brezhnev's warnings of impending war between Arabs and Israelis as a negotiating ploy; Kissinger remained unmoved even after the Soviets began to ferry diplomatic personnel and their families out of Arab states. Of course, following the outbreak of hostilities and the uptick in oil prices, the Soviet Union reaped benefits far greater than anything détente had delivered. Inside the Kremlin, the earlier anxiety about the negative effects of a Middle East war must have seemed comical.

But history was playing a cruel trick. Since the 1930s the Soviet Union had rapidly industrialized, captured Hitler's Berlin, launched Sputnik, banged its shoe on the podium of the UN, and boasted that it would bury capitalism. But by winning the Second World War, and therefore having no necessity, or feeling no desire, to change fundamentally to compete in the transformed post-war international context, the Soviet Union in a way doomed itself. Not only did it suffer a crushing turnaround *outside* the country between the 1930s and the 1960s, but also, right in the midst of its great 1970s oil boom, the socialist revolution entered a decrepit old age.

Soviet economic growth slowed substantially, and,

because quality was notoriously poor, requiring high rates of replacement, a Soviet economy growing at 2 per cent was tantamount to stagnation. Soon, outright recession—by official statistics—set in. Decades of ecological degradation also reached the tipping point. Key demographic trends were reversed: infant mortality began to rise, and life expectancy at birth began to decline. These negative data were covered up or falsified, but, for the huge populations in the Soviet Union's industrial toxic zones, there was no concealing the fact that respiratory ailments among children had become epidemic, that the incidence of cancer grew phenomenally, and that alcoholism and absenteeism, already high, were rising. Behind this deep domestic funk, lay the fact that the competition with capitalism—not a policy, but something inherent to the system's identity and survival—was unwinnable.

The 1973 oil shock initially had seemed to doom capitalism's remarkable post-war run, but it definitively pushed capitalism further on to a path of deep structural reforms. Those changes would soon cast the USSR's greatest ostensible achievement—its hyper fossil-fuel economy, upon which its superpower status rested—into a time warp, which its institutional framework could not or would not manage to confront. The 1980s decline in Soviet oil output and in world oil prices made the pain immediate. But it was by no means a foregone conclusion that the full intractability of these profound structural weaknesses would be exposed to the world and the inhabitants of the Soviet Union. What suddenly exposed, and vastly accelerated, the Soviet system's decline in the mid and late 1980s was an unavoidable generational change at the top, followed by a much-anticipated campaign to reinvigorate the socialist system. That of course was Mikhail Gorbachev's ill-fated perestroika.

In his 1987 book *Perestroika*, which sold five million copies in eighty languages, Gorbachev defined his programme as 'an urgent necessity'. But the Brezhnev leadership had ignored or downplayed the increasing imbalances with the US, and after his death the country could have continued on the same path. Relative to the West, the planned economy performed inadequately, but it employed nearly every person of working age, and the Soviet standard of living, though disappointing, was tolerable for most people (given what they did not know owing to censorship and travel restrictions). The Soviet Union was not in turmoil. Nationalist separatism existed, but it did not remotely threaten the Soviet order. The KGB crushed the small dissident movement. The enormous intelligentsia griped incessantly, but it enjoyed massive state subsidies manipulated to promote overall loyalty. Respect for the army was extremely high. Soviet patriotism was very strong. Soviet nuclear forces could have annihilated the world many times over. Only the unravelling of the socialist system in Poland constituted an immediate danger, but even that was put off by the successful 1981 Polish crackdown.

Perestroika, however, was born not simply in tangible indicators, but in the crucial psychological dimension of the superpower competition.[14] Among Soviet elites, there was panic at the scope of Western advances as well as humiliation at the country's deepening relative backwardness. There were, in addition, unmistakable signs of internal defection in elite ranks. By the 1970s and early 1980s, large swathes of the Soviet Union's upper ranks, including academics, were travelling to the West, and, whether patriots or cynics, they usually came back loaded down with boom boxes, VCRs, fancy clothes, and other goods. The highest officials had such items discretely imported for them, while their children, the future generation of Soviet leadership, pursued coveted long-term postings abroad in the not very socialist occupation of foreign trade representatives. Many party posts, which served as vehicles for enrichment, were being sold to the highest bidder. In 1982, one émigré defector derided the USSR as a 'land of kleptocracy'.[15] Soulless indulgence, on top of a loss of confidence, had taken deep root, and this frightened loyalists most of all.

Socialist idealism

How does a dictatorship, particularly one without even the discipline of private property and a strong judiciary necessitated by a market economy, control proliferating ranks of its own functionaries? After 1953, when Stalin died, mass terror ceased to be practicable, and anyway it had never prevented malfeasance. In the ensuing decades,

Soviet leaders continued to struggle trying to curb the behaviour of officials. Khrushchev relied upon client networks and toyed with possible term limits for party posts before being ousted. Brezhnev also favoured clientelism, pitting ever-growing informal 'family circles', or groupings of officials, against each other, but he proclaimed a post-Stalin 'stability of cadres', which became an invitation to licentiousness. Andropov launched campaigns to tighten discipline, and dozens of death sentences were handed out for bribe taking or the abuse of authority, but the overwhelming majority of official misdeeds went unpunished. How could it have been otherwise? In the fulfilment of tasks, rule violations were not only condoned but also encouraged, and determining which violations were permissible, to what degree, and in which circumstances, was arbitrary. If every transgression were to have been punished, almost all of Soviet officialdom would have had to have been executed or jailed.[16]

All of this was well known, of course, but many party officials nonetheless retained considerable faith in the possibilities of socialism and the party itself. Indeed, the party, not just the economy, was the target of perestroika. And the party was, simultaneously, also the instrument of perestroika. Gorbachev, as well as the like-minded officials and academic advisers he assembled around him, was acutely aware of the dramatic changes in the post-war West, and the historical fork in the world economy that had popped up in the 1970s—what they called the scientific-technological revolution. Yet they still considered their country to be on a different time line, for which the key dates were: 1917, the October revolution; 1924, Lenin's death, followed by Stalin's 'usurpation'; 1956, the beginning of Khrushchev's drive for reform socialism; 1964, Khrushchev's sacking; and 1968, the Prague Spring's suppression, which trampled, but did not lay to rest, the vision of a humane socialism. It was not just the superpower competition but a deeply felt urge to make socialism live up to its promises, to reinvigorate the party and return to the imagined ideals of October, that shaped both the decision to launch perestroika and, even more importantly, the *specific form* it took.

In a delicious irony, very rigid political and concomitant economic structures were shaken to their foundations by what was erroneously assumed to have been the Soviet Union's most rigid structure, Communist ideology. Marxism-Leninism, after a generational change, turned out to be the source of extraordinary, albeit destabilizing, dynamism. What proved to be the party's final mobilization, perestroika, was driven not by cold calculation about achieving an orderly retrenchment, but by the pursuit of a romantic dream.

2

Reviving the dream

We are firmly of the opinion that in the course of peaceful competition the peoples will be able to satisfy themselves as to which social system secures them a higher standard of living, greater assurance for the future, freer access to education and culture, more perfect forms of democracy and personal freedom. We have no doubt that in such competition Communism will win.

(Nikita Khrushchev, preface, *New Communist Party Programme*, 1961)

Gorbachev, unlike Brezhnev, strikes me as a true believer.

(Milovan Djilas, 1988)

Russia's chaotic, wartime 1917 revolutions were propelled by a desire to remake the world, to overcome what was perceived to be the country's false and hideous life, and achieve a just and beautiful life, through mass violence if necessary. By the 1930s, under Stalin, the revolutionary dream for a world of abundance without exploitation had become an enslavement of the peasantry and a forced, headlong expansion of heavy industry, with millions of people called upon to sacrifice whatever it took to 'catch and overtake' the capitalists. Alongside the roar of heavy industry, there was also the stamping of jackboots: the Imperial Japanese over-running Manchuria; the Italian fascists marching through Abyssinia (Ethiopia); the Nazis annexing Austria and the Czech lands. The Soviet regime consumed the country and itself in terror, but also girded itself in the armour of advanced modernity—blast furnaces, turbines, tanks, airplanes—and mobilized its hardened factory workers, collective farmers, camp inmates, and commissars for war.

The Second World War was a defining moment for the Soviet Union. No other industrial country has ever experienced the devastation that befell the USSR *in victory*. The Nazi onslaught of 1941–5 levelled more than 1,700 Soviet towns and 70,000 villages, and obliterated about one-third of the USSR's wealth. Soviet military deaths numbered at least seven million, about half the total for all combatants (the Germans lost 3.5 million soldiers; the Americans about 300,000). Soviet civilian deaths probably numbered between seventeen and twenty million, making its combined human losses near twenty-seven million. Almost an equal number of people were left homeless. Another two million perished from famine between 1946 and 1948. Each year of the first post-war decade, approximately one million children were born out of wedlock, as women unable to find husbands took initiative. Even so, the 1941 pre-invasion population of 200 million was not reached again until 1956. The war was an enduring catastrophe.

Politically, the war broke the regime-imposed isolation. Millions of Red Army soldiers advanced beyond Soviet borders, and most were stunned by what they saw. 'I was a member of the Communist party, I was an officer in the Red Army,' wrote Peter Gornev. But 'in Finland, Poland, and Germany, I saw that most people were better off than we were. Soviet propaganda had told us just the reverse. The Soviet government had always lied to us. Now I had a chance to escape from the lies.'[1] Here was the classic disillusionment story, better known from the anthology 'the God that failed'.[2] Among displaced Soviet subjects like Gornev, a few hundred thousand avoided return. But more than three million were repatriated from the US, French, and British occupation zones of Germany. This substantial population with first-hand experience of the outside world frightened the Soviet leadership. Even returning POWs and slave labourers, who somehow managed to survive German captivity, were made to pass through special screening; many disappeared in the Soviet camp complex colloquially known as the Gulag.

Western annexations, following the Red Army advance, meant that several million people who had not lived under the Soviet regime during the 'heroic' 1930s mobilizations to build socialism found themselves incorporated into the USSR. Mass deportations sought to quell opposition among them, but in the Baltic republics and western Ukraine partisans sustained guerrilla wars through the late 1940s and early 1950s. By this time, large-scale mutinies rocked the Gulag, which held close to three million convicts in labour camps alone, more than one-third incarcerated for political crimes, the rest for so-called common crimes (theft, drunkenness, rape, murder). Protesting camp inmates had engaged in hand-to-hand combat in the defence of Stalingrad; now serving twenty-five-year terms, they were not afraid of much. Shouting slogans such as 'Long Live the Soviet Constitution!', they demanded an eight-hour work day, unrestricted correspondence with family members, periodic visits, and judicial review of cases. They were strafed by Soviet warplanes.

Few inhabitants inside the Soviet Union learned of the revolts in the Gulag or of the forest-dwelling anti-Soviet partisans. What they did know was that the country had withstood the Nazi war machine. Many hoped changes and a better life would follow. Unsolicited reform proposals poured forth, advocating competition among enterprises and private trade, but they were relegated to the archives.[3] Victorious, the Soviet dictatorship felt no imperative to change, and fell back upon familiar patterns of bureaucratic hyper-centralization and economics by command. Propagandists exhorted the weary populace to rebuild the country, which they did, brick by brick, despite the harangues. The state media revived the pre-war theme of hostile capitalist encirclement, and relentlessly demonized the West, casting Soviet deprivation, once again, as a matter of heroic sacrifice. Heavy industry, as in the 1930s, received the bulk of investment, and the country regained—and, by 1950, surpassed—its pre-war Fordist-style industrial base. It also exploded its own atomic bomb. Stalin's death in 1953 was a psychological blow, but Nikita Khrushchev's de-Stalinization campaign, launched in 1956, seemed to reinvigorate the system. The dream of the socialist revolution—to 'catch and overtake' the most advanced countries and, in the process, build a better, more just world—rose from the ashes for a new generation.

The education of a true believer

Born in 1931 in a village in Stavropol province, a fertile land of Russia's multi-ethnic North Caucasus, Mikhail Gorbachev experienced a life trajectory resembling that of millions of his compatriots: a middling-peasant family background; the somersault of the rural social order with collectivization; the (brief) deportation to Siberia of his grandfather; the arrest (and release) in the Great Terror of his other grandfather, the local collective-farm chairman; the Second World War front for his father (who was wounded but survived); and the Nazi occupation for the elderly, women, and children, like young Mikhail, left behind in the village. After the war, Gorbachev might have become a farmer, like his father and grandfather, but Stalin's upheavals—besides arrests and famine—brought educational opportunities. Graduating from high school in 1950, Gorbachev set his sights not on the provincial university but on Moscow. With a peasant-worker background, a pupil's silver medal for a nearly perfect record, and a very high state award—the Order of the Red Banner—for helping bring in the 1948 bumper harvest, he was accepted, and made the leap to the Soviet capital.

That late Stalin-era Moscow University could have opened a youth's mind may appear implausible. During his five years at Moscow State University's law faculty, then located across from the Kremlin, the Stavropol hayseed came into contact with a handful of erudite professors, some educated before the revolution, married a fetching philosophy student whom he had met at a class on ballroom dancing, and joined the Communist Party. Acknowledging his personal anguish midway through his college years over Stalin's death, Gorbachev explains that, immersed as he was in the leaden Stalinist atmosphere, poring over the lively, polemical works of Marx and Lenin proved liberating, and taught him critical analytical skills. He also recalls the heady access to Moscow's cultural elite, and the backbreaking summers at home on the collective farm. Inevitably, yet no doubt with theoretical conviction, his senior thesis argued the advantages of socialism over capitalism.

As a law-faculty graduate (1955), Gorbachev was assigned to the public prosecutor's office in Stavropol, which, although a provincial capital, lacked a central water supply or sewage system. He found a tiny room to rent only after a colleague let him in on what all the prosecutors did: use their rap sheets to contact an illegal apartment broker. Having immediately been compelled to violate the law for his own benefit, and become acquainted with the Stalin-era personnel who dominated the provincial 'law' agencies, the Moscow-educated Gorbachev soon abandoned the prosecutor's office for an organization that offered career advancement and a chance to realize himself: the Communist Youth League (Komsomol). He set about travelling to remote settlements and organizing discussion groups 'to fling open a window onto the world'.[4] The next year, Khrushchev delivered his 'secret speech' at the Twentieth Party Congress, enumerating Stalin's crimes. The revelations divided the country into those who defended Stalin and those who condemned him, often because their families, like Gorbachev's, had been victimized, but also because the anti-Stalin campaign promised a fresh start on the path to the bright future.

Gorbachev was 25 when shown a copy of Khrushchev's unpublished text, and on the verge of being named first secretary of the local Komsomol. Tanks were sent to quell a revolt in socialist Hungary, but the Soviet press cited a threat of counter-revolution and capitalist intervention. The stunning October 1957 launch of Sputnik, the world's first man-made satellite, confirmed the Soviet post-war resurrection, and its commitment to science and education. The tropical crowds of the surprise 1959 Cuban revolution evoked for a visiting Soviet delegation their own revolution in 1917.[5] In September of 1960,

Khrushchev thundered from the podium of the United Nations, 'History is on our side. We will bury you.' In 1961 another Soviet rocket lifted cosmonaut Yuri Gagarin into space, and he returned to earth safely. The Twenty-Second Party Congress—attended by Gorbachev—approved a new party programme heralding a transition from socialism to history's next and final stage, Communism by 1980, within the lifetimes of his generation.[6]

Back in Stavropol, pressure to bring home a bigger harvest only intensified, yet Khrushchev's multiple administrative reorganizations and campaigns caused disruption and brought mixed results. In Moscow, his proposal of term limits for apparatchiks stiffened some backs, and in October 1964 he was 'retired' in a conspiracy. No tanks, no riots, no executions—and no let-up in the imperious demands to fulfil plan targets for local officials, such as Gorbachev, who in 1962 had been transferred from the youth league to the party apparat. Just eight years later, he became—at age 39—party chief for the entire province. Though still a provincial, he had joined the top elite, and took his first trips to 'bourgeois' countries, driving with his wife through much of France and Italy—a world away from the Soviet Union. Taken aback by the standard of living and civic freedoms, Gorbachev writes that he returned still convinced public education and medical services were organized 'more fairly in our country'. At the same time, the staggering wealth gap brought home the urgency to 'catch up'.[7]

Just as eye opening, Gorbachev was sent to Czechoslovakia for an 'exchange of views' on youth issues in 1969, right after the Soviet crackdown. He was able to see that, contrary to the Kremlin line, the Soviet presence amounted to an occupation, since his 'fraternal' delegation required round-the-clock guards. That same year, also as if by fate, Yuri Andropov, chairman of the KGB, visited an elite spa town of Stavropol province for kidney treatment, and Gorbachev played host. The two struck up a relationship that deepened on Andropov's subsequent rest cures. It was the KGB chief who engineered both the pulverization of the Prague Spring and the promotion, in November 1978, of the earnest provincial to Moscow as the Central Committee (CC) secretary for agriculture. Unexpectedly, the country's top post in Gorbachev's speciality had become vacant only because its occupant, Fyodor Kulakov—also from Stavropol, and considered a possible successor to Brezhnev—died at age 60 of an alcohol overdose while recovering from stomach surgery.[8] Just 47, Gorbachev became by far the youngest member of the Kremlin leadership, most of whom had been born around 1910. The generation in between—that of 1920—had been largely decimated in the war.

Creeping invasion of the West

During the twenty-three years (1955–78) that Gorbachev had worked his way up and commanded the province of Stavropol, Soviet society had changed profoundly.

Two-thirds of the population had lived in villages when Gorbachev was born, but by the late 1970s townspeople outnumbered country folk by almost two to one. And whereas, towards the end of Stalin's time, most urbanites still lived in barracks or 'communal apartments', sharing kitchen and bath with other tenants, under Brezhnev more than half the growing city population lived in apartments with private baths and kitchens. Millions of families were also able to build modest country retreats (dachas) with vegetable gardens. Between 1970 and 1978 the number of domestic vacationers at sanatoria and resorts jumped from 16 million to 35 million, while another one million per year travelled to Eastern Europe. By this time, more than 90 per cent of Soviet families owned refrigerators, more than 60 per cent owned washing machines.

There were significantly more goods than before, yet much of the Soviet population queued for hours to obtain basic necessities and had to turn to the more expensive 'shadow economy' of informal production and exchange for children's clothes, proper-sized adult shoes, and other scarce items. That was because consumer goods production lagged behind military and heavy industry, and central planning empowered producers, not consumers. Similarly, no matter how joyous people were when moving into a new prefabricated apartment, usually after waiting ten years, their space was invariably insufficient—one, two, or at most three rooms for husband, wife, children, grandparents. The authorities just could not keep up.

And, although people had more, they were demanding more, on the basis of wider horizons. Back in 1950, the year Gorbachev had entered Moscow University, there were 1.25 million students enrolled in higher education, about 3 per cent of the population, but by the late 1970s, fully 10 per cent of the Soviet population had completed college. About 70 per cent had completed high school, compared with 40 per cent in 1950.

Mass media technologies—motion pictures, radio—had long been important in the Soviet dictatorship's ability to disseminate the kinds of information and ways of interpreting the world it deemed appropriate. These remained powerful state levers, but over time foreign content increasingly entered the stream of mass culture in the Soviet Union, notwithstanding censorship. Into the 1950s, Soviet radios meant a wire hooked up to a feed bringing one or two stations from Moscow, rather than wave receivers, but, by the late 1960s, wave radios came to exceed wire ones, and the total number of all radios grew to nearly ninety million (from around eighteen million at Stalin's death). Technical adepts reconfigured Soviet-manufactured radios to receive short wave from abroad, broadcast as part of the cold war. True, a good part of state radio facilities were busy producing static to cover up Radio Liberty, BBC, Deutsche Welle, and Voice of America, which collectively were known as 'the voices'. Yet listeners could escape jamming out in the country and learn the forbidden details of Soviet political life and world events.

In this creeping post-war cultural invasion of the USSR by the West, an even more important role was played by images and details of consumerism, some of which were being delivered by a new and quintessential mass medium, television. The number of Soviet TV sets leapt from 400 in 1940, to 2.5 million in 1958, thirty million ten years later, and ninety million in the 1980s, by which time they could be found in 93 per cent of households. Post-war programmes began to focus on home life, and, beginning in the mid-1970s, the authorities permitted translations of family serials from Britain (*The Forsyte Saga, David Copperfield*), France (*Les Thibaults*), and other capitalist countries. Such shows, like the increasingly available foreign films, were watched as much for clues of material life as for entertainment. Soviet audiences would intently observe the characters moving through well-furnished homes from one room to another room and then another room, sometimes eight or more in all. The characters also appeared in different clothes each day, peered into over-stuffed refrigerators, and drove sleek cars. It was all fantasy—or was it?

Certainly, Soviet television was dominated by official views, and in general control over communications remained very tight. Private telephones were kept to a minimum—twenty-five million, fewer than one for every ten people—and typewriters had to be registered with the police. Access to photocopiers was tightly restricted. But tape recorders, owned by about one-third of the population, as well as cheap X-ray plates (pressed as LPs), facilitated the circulation of forbidden Soviet popular bal-lads as well as smuggled rock and roll. In 1968, ostensibly to combat worrisome trends in youth culture, Komsomol officials gathered at a retreat to watch the officially banned film *Easy Rider*. Soon, almost every Soviet high school and factory acquired its own rock-and-roll band, which the Komsomol hired to perform at official events. By the late Brezhnev era, Soviet public spaces were decor-ated not just with official slogans but also with graffiti about sports teams, rock music, sex, and the merits of punk music versus heavy metal. Schoolchildren 'ranked' each other by their jeans, with Western brands being the highest.

This infatuation with the Western consumer culture was a far cry from the heroic October revolution and Civil War, the 1930s building of socialism, or the Second World War, which had shaped earlier generations. Despite prominent post-war campaigns to settle 'virgin lands' and build a sec-ond railroad through Siberia, it was clear that the mobili-zational style of political participation and socialization was losing much of its force. Equally important, the party's grand historical teleology had to be abandoned. As the predicted date of 1980 for the transition to Communism passed, ideologues replaced Khrushchev's utopian prom-ise with the here and now of 'developed' socialism.[9] Was life simply a question of washing machines, refrigerators, private cars, TVs, popular music, and jeans, and, if so, what did that portend for socialism's struggle against capitalism?

Abiding allegiance to socialism

Even as the Soviet population began to sense the prosperity gap with the US, Japan, and Western Europe, the overwhelming majority still responded to the incessant propaganda about the Soviet Union's lack of unemployment, gulf between rich and poor, race riots, or Vietnam War. Mass construction of self-contained apartments had given rise to the celebrated urban ritual of the 'kitchen table', where Soviet families and trusted friends assembled out of earshot of nosy neighbours and the authorities to discuss the absurdities of their lives. Indeed, jokes about the Soviet system became something of a private and sometimes public activity, and very little love was lost on apparatchiks. But, beyond desiring a degree of liberalization, most people simply wanted the Soviet regime to live up to its promises of inexpensive housing, health care, paid maternity leave, public education, and consumer goods. A strong allegiance to socialism—understood as state responsibility for the general welfare and social justice—remained very much a part of ordinary people's world view, confirmed by such facts as the near impossibility of being evicted from their state-provided apartments, whatever the circumstances.[10]

Substantial legitimacy for socialism was also derived from the commemoration of the Second World War in films, memoirs, veterans groups, and monuments, all of which, like military-patriotic education, were expanded in the 1960s. The main Soviet holiday, Revolution Day

(7 November), became a showcase for Soviet military hardware, though for many it was noteworthy for the extra consumer goods and alcohol made available. But Victory Day (9 May) was a powerful collective ritual, involving family trips to the cemetery, whose meaning was shared by almost the entire country. Victory Day also underscored the attainment of superpower status and reinforced the respect for the Armed Forces. Of course, coercion remained an integral aspect of maintaining allegiance. 'The KGB was a repressive, not an educational organ,' wrote Filipp Bobkov, a veteran of forty-five years who rose to become first deputy chairman. 'Nonetheless, we tried, when possible, to use prophylactic measures,' meaning summoning individuals to local KGB headquarters, and blackmailing them to inform on their colleagues.[11] Many people collaborated with the authorities' requests without much pressure, and more than a few came forward on their own.

The KGB, like the Western media, was obsessed over manifestations of what it regarded as non-conformist behaviour. But of the several thousand individuals jailed or exiled for unorthodox views or actions during the Brezhnev years, only a small minority consisted of internationally recognized human-rights campaigners such as the physicist Andrei Sakharov, who won the Nobel Peace Prize (in 1975). A second category of dissenters comprised hard-core separatists, especially in western regions annexed during the 1940s. But seekers of religious freedom constituted the great majority of those who suffered at the hands of the regime; there were seventeen attempts at self-immolation on Red Square in 1981 alone, none of them known to the outside world, and more importantly, to the Soviet population.[12] A leader of Moscow's underground human-rights organization, summing up the situation in 1984, wrote, 'the history of dissent in the USSR is a tragic one', adding correctly that 'the movement never became a mass movement and the immediate demands of the dissidents were almost wholly frustrated'.[13]

But the regime faced a threat considerably greater than 'dissidents': a several-million-strong army of scientists who were overwhelmingly not politically active yet still clashed with the authorities because they needed access to basic domestic data—let alone foreign publications—which were denied to them by their hack political supervisors. This dilemma of needing and yet stifling scientific exchange became ever more acute, and a few top apparatchiks broached the possibility of relaxing censorship. But the party's chief ideologue in the Brezhnev period, Mikhail Suslov—a CC secretary since 1949 (under Stalin), and a full politburo member since 1955—pointed out that it was only a matter of months after the removal of censorship in Czechoslovakia that the tanks had to roll in. Who, he asked, was going to send tanks to the Soviet Union? Some restrictions were eased on a case-by-case basis, but for most scientists, just as for cultural intellectuals, Communist Party membership was a prerequisite for career advancement, and was used to enforce the basic chain of command.

Outside Moscow, republic party machines, usually led by a Communist of the titular nation, with a Russian as number two, received substantial autonomy in exchange for maintaining loyalty to Moscow. National themes did become ever more prevalent in the non-Russian republics, paralleling the 'national Communism' of Eastern Europe, but nationalism was nowhere allowed to displace the official socialist ideology, and loyalty was nowhere in question. Only in the Russian republic—which alone lacked a separate republic party—were Russian nationalists permitted, occasionally, to criticize Marxist-Leninism and atheism publicly in the name of the preservation of pre-revolutionary monuments, the Russian soul, and the environment.[14] But such cultural nationalism was never allowed to become an independent force. In both Russia and the non-Russian republics, separatist threats were weak, and multinational solidarity strong, reinforced by propaganda, Russification and its career advantages, the mutual dependencies of the planned economy, and the high incidence of ethnically mixed marriages. Russian dominated, and replete with injustices, the Union fostered many resentments, but, rather than a cauldron of mutually exclusive nationalisms, it was in many ways a polyglot, multicultural world.

In sum, the post-war Soviet Union tried to slake a thirst for self-contained apartments that gave people some private space, provided educational opportunities that made people both orthodox and critical, and expanded communications technologies, letting in more of the Western world. The authorities encountered a sharpening divergence between the aims of advancing science and maintaining secrecy for political reasons. They were also unable to energize society, especially youth, with the antiquated model of heroic mobilization, or to satisfy a growing restlessness, bordering on a sense of entitlement. But they drew upon pride in the Second World War victory, and expediently allowed nationalisms to mix with Communism, while retaining censorship. Overall, these post-war developments were not remarkable in themselves. They were, however, made *potentially* very dangerous by the economic boom, consumer revolution, mass cultural explosion, and embrace of democracy *outside* the USSR.

Direct access to life in the West was granted only to select members of the Soviet upper ranks. No less restricted was access to the lives of those higher strata. Elite hospitals, resorts, supply networks, and schools were closed affairs; even the maids of the elite were usually KGB employees who reported on their masters' lives only for secret dossiers. Russia's socialist revolution, having originated in a radical quest for egalitarianism, produced an insulated privileged class increasingly preoccupied with the spoils of office for themselves and their children. The existence of a vast and self-indulgent elite was the greatest contradiction in the post-war Soviet Union, and the most volatile.

Jockeying invalids

At the very top, where decisions were concentrated, the Soviet elite was growing old and infirm. Leonid Brezhnev first became ill in 1968 during the crisis over Czechoslovakia, when he took too many sleeping pills. He had worked tenaciously to obtain an about-face by the Czechoslovak leadership, but finally sent in the tanks.[15] The Soviet leader developed insomnia, though otherwise he functioned normally. Those who met him in the late 1960s and early 1970s came away impressed with his political skills. In November 1974, however, Brezhnev suffered a major stroke. A second stroke, which left him clinically dead for a time, followed in January 1976. Later that year, in the months leading up to his seventieth birthday, he had several heart attacks. Both at the end of 1974 and in 1976 there were hints of a possible retirement.[16] Instead, *after* the onset of Brezhnev's debilitating illness, supreme rule was consolidated by a tight-knit Brezhnevite clique.

Between 1977 and 1980, those whom Brezhnev considered rivals were removed. The general secretary added the title of Supreme Soviet chairman, while giving the government to a trusted apparatchik, Nikolai Tikhonov. In two other moves, Dmitry Ustinov, the defence minister, and Konstantin Chernenko, a Brezhnev protégé over decades, became politburo members. This faction—Ustinov (defence), Chernenko (party apparat), and Tikhonov (economy), with the support of Andropov (KGB), the primordial Suslov (ideology), and the long-serving Andrei

Gromyko (foreign minister)—exercised unlimited power in their domains by keeping the enfeebled Brezhnev in place. They were perpetually briefed on the country's myriad problems, but remained unsympathetic to proposals for major reforms, especially after the distasteful experience of 1968 Czechoslovakia; anyway, oil money was flowing into Kremlin coffers.[17]

Just as the Brezhnevite faction was taking shape, the much younger Mikhail Gorbachev, having knocked himself out to reach the inner sanctum, achieved his ambition, only to come face to face with the system's paralysis. Brezhnev, incoherent from arteriosclerosis and tranquillizer overdoses, worked no more than two hours a day, and politburo meetings often lasted just twenty minutes. Even after the general secretary began drooling on himself in appearances on Soviet television, the clique around him took no action, other than to nominate him for still more medals. While Brezhnev acquired more state awards than all previous Soviet leaders *combined*, and more military awards than Marshal Zhukov, who had captured Berlin, the leadership's average age surpassed 70. In late 1979 the narrow ruling group enmeshed the Soviet Union in a war in neighbouring Afghanistan (nominally to protect a client), without properly informing the rest of the elite, let alone the people. The Soviet political system had no mechanisms for self-correction.

In the wider world, computers were revolutionizing communications, services were forming an increasing share of economic activity, manufacturing was being transformed by flexible production, and cross-border capital flows were escalating, penetrating even Eastern Europe. Japan had become an economic colossus on the basis of high-value-added exports. East Asia also saw the emergence of the 'Four Tigers', Hong Kong, Singapore, Taiwan, and South Korea, whose GDP had been as low as Ghana's as recently as the early 1960s. In China, the elderly Communist leadership, while maintaining a firm grip on central power, sanctioned a move to the market throughout the countryside and in urban areas of select coastal provinces. Denouncing China's 'capitalist road' deviationism, Moscow fell into a recession in 1980. A decree announcing a Soviet economic reform was published the year before, but no concrete measures followed.

Finally, in January 1982, the 79-year-old Suslov—the party's unofficial number two, but a man who had not aspired to the top job—triggered a succession struggle by dying. Brezhnev, himself on death's door, moved the 68-year-old Andropov from the KGB to Suslov's office in the CC Secretariat, but allowed his own main minder, the 70-year-old Chernenko, to perform Suslov's duties of chairing the Secretariat. The two invalids jockeyed for power until November 1982, when Brezhnev died. Andropov, supported by Ustinov, became general secretary. Gromyko privately suggested himself as second secretary (and putative successor), but that honour fell on the wheezing Chernenko. It all was just intrigue. No Brezhnev succession had taken place. Nationally, much hope was placed in

Andropov, who was seen as a vigorous leader, but after just three months at the helm, he became bedridden. By the autumn of 1983, his lungs and liver, on top of his kidneys, had ceased working.

Sick as he was, Andropov managed to put in place a new potential ruling team. Evidently seeing the uncorrupt, close-to-the-soil Gorbachev as the man who could 'bear our hopes into the future', Andropov instructed his protégé while he was still CC secretary for agriculture to assume responsibility for the entire economy.[18] To back Gorbachev up, Andropov transferred Nikolai Ryzhkov from Gosplan to a newly revamped economics department within the CC Secretariat. Andropov also summoned Yegor Ligachev, a Gorbachev acquaintance, from western Siberia to take charge of the critical CC department for personnel. Ligachev, an acclaimed arm-twister, writes that he assumed 'the unpleasant mission' of apprising numerous officials of their enforced retirements, while Gorbachev informed those to be promoted.[19] With Andropov having lost every bodily function except his mind, whispers of a Gorbachev succession brushed the corridors of power. In February 1984, Andropov fell into a coma and died.

Behind the scenes, Ustinov, Tikhonov, and Gromyko rallied around Chernenko, by then an invalid dying of emphysema. Gorbachev was crestfallen, but Chernenko tapped him to become number two and chair the Secretariat. At the politburo meeting to rubber stamp the recommendation, however, the 80-year-old Tikhonov

pointedly asked if there were no other candidates. Someone else suggested they could all rotate. The 75-year-old
Gromyko, appearing the conciliator, proposed that, since
there was disagreement, the question should be postponed. Gorbachev was not allowed to move into
Chernenko's (and Suslov's) old office, and was never
confirmed as second secretary. He performed the duties
anyway, including chairing politburo meetings when
Chernenko became bedridden. Thus, despite the intrigues, the Andropov-assembled Gorbachev–Ligachev–
Ryzhkov team remained in place. But the old guard held
on, reduced—after the December 1984 death of
Ustinov—to the triumvirate of Chernenko, Tikhonov,
and Gromyko. The trio had a concealed escalator built so
they could still ascend Lenin's mausoleum for holiday
parades.

'We were ashamed of our state, of its half-dead leaders,
of the encroaching senility,' recalled Nikolai Leonov, then
a top analyst of the post-war generation in the KGB, which
since the 1970s had been preparing memoranda for an
indifferent politburo on the widening technological gap
with the West, increasing alcoholism at home (with
attendant crime, low productivity, and birth defects), and
the unsustainability of global adventurism.

Many a time we discussed these questions in a circle of the
closest colleagues . . . We all sincerely and unshakeably believed
in socialism as a higher and more humane system than capitalism. We were also convinced that all our troubles derived
from the so-called subjective factor—the personal qualities

of our leaders. We hoped and believed that a new, young, anointed generation of party and state leaders would come to power.[20]

The unavoidable generational shift

On 10 March 1985 at 7.20 p.m., Chernenko, after having been in a coma, died. First to be notified by the Kremlin doctor was Gorbachev, who instructed the apparat to convene a politburo meeting that same evening at 11:00. The man rumoured to be Gorbachev's principal rival, Viktor Grishin, the head of the powerful Moscow city party committee and an intimate of Chernenko, learned of Chernenko's death from Gorbachev. Provocatively, Gorbachev suggested to Grishin that the latter should chair Chernenko's funeral commission. In the past, the funeral commission chair had always become the general secretary. Grishin demurred, proposing that Gorbachev be chair. The message was clear: Grishin did not have the forces to challenge Gorbachev. But at the politburo meeting itself, with top position finally within his grasp, Gorbachev brushed aside a motion by Grishin to be named funeral commission chairman. No one else was nominated. Strangely, no vote was taken.[21]

The succession seemed, that night, still up in the air. But it was not. As *de facto* Secretariat chief, Gorbachev assumed responsibility for arranging the funeral, the next day's afternoon meeting of the politburo, and the same day's follow-up plenary session of the CC; indeed, it was Gorbachev who had decided to call the initial politburo meeting. Together with Yegor Ligachev and KGB Chairman Viktor Chebrikov, Gorbachev worked at party HQ until the wee small hours. Later that morning, 11 March, prior to the second politburo session, Gromyko suddenly telephoned Ligachev to indicate he would back Gorbachev. As was agreed, at the second politburo meeting Gromyko dramatically stood up, pre-empting the others, and, like a kingmaker, nominated Gorbachev for general secretary. Tikhonov seconded the nomination. Fifteen others tripped over each other to concur. At the CC gathering that would formally vote on the politburo's recommendation, Gromyko again stood up first, and his disclosure of the choice for Gorbachev drew resounding applause.

Could the outcome have turned out differently? Was there a succession struggle?

Back in 1978, when Andropov had contrived Gorbachev's transfer into the inner circle, the next youngest CC secretary was Chernenko, twenty years Gorbachev's senior. Inevitably, the gerontocrats began to die off: Suslov (1982), Brezhnev (1982), Andropov (1983), Ustinov (1984), and Chernenko (1985). In March 1985, the two surviving elder statesmen, Tikhonov and Gromyko, both entertained notions of their own candidacy.[22] But, even if one had agreed to step aside for the other, age considerations would have dictated only another Chernenko-like interregnum. Slightly less senior men—notably the 70-year-old Grishin—had made no secret of their aspirations. But Grishin was dogged by charges of corruption.[23] His nomination of the 54-year-old Gorbachev to chair the funeral commission demonstrated that the latter held all the cards: the mantle of Andropov, the *de facto* directorship of the crucial party Secretariat, the weighty logistical support of the KGB, and relative youth. Why, then, would Gorbachev not have leapt at Grishin's motion the first night to become funeral commission chairman, settling the question immediately? It seems his ego was waiting on the purely formal blessing of the old guard, above all Gromyko.

In his memoirs Gorbachev does not even mention the supposedly decisive next morning phone call of support from Gromyko. What he does disclose is that the previous evening, twenty minutes prior to the politburo's first meeting, he had arranged a secret *tête-à-tête* with Gromyko, but the senior figure remained noncommittal.[24] *Gromyko's 'waffling' was the entire 'succession struggle'.* In the two years following Andropov's death, Gromyko had schemed to sustain his own impossible chances by joining forces with Tikhonov, who engaged in all manner of nasty tricks, such as blocking a confirmation vote of Gorbachev's status as second secretary under Chernenko, and instigating a covert search for compromising material on Gorbachev's days in Stavropol. But these desperate manœuvrings could have little effect, other than ruining Gorbachev's nerves. He was the lone representative of a younger generation in the politburo, and ultimately a generational change could not be avoided.

Unlike the septugenarians and octogenarians of the ever-narrowing inner circle, the former country bumpkin from Stavropol—the youngest Soviet leader since Stalin—would prove to be a tactical virtuoso. Even more unlike the men he replaced, Gorbachev would show himself to be resolutely committed to renewing socialist ideals. All this may make him appear highly unusual. But belief in a better socialism marked most 'children' of the party's 1956 Twentieth Congress. Gorbachev's beliefs, as well as his supreme self-confidence, were only deepened by first-hand experience of the men who had consolidated their power around the infirm Brezhnev (and then, one by one, filled urns in the Kremlin wall cemetery). Far from an aberration, Gorbachev was a quintessential product of the Soviet system, and a faithful representative of the system's trajectory as it entered the second half of the 1980s. His cohort hailed him as the long-awaited 'reformer', a second Khrushchev. They were right. Belief in a humane socialism had re-emerged from within the system, and this time, in even more politically skilful hands, it would prove fatal.

3

The drama of reform

I don't understand how we can fight the Communist
Party under the leadership of the Communist Party
... I don't understand why perestroika is being
carried out by the same people who brought the
country to the point where it needs perestroika.

(Mikhail Zadornov, Russian satirist, 1989)

Liberalization and democratization are in essence
counter-revolution.

(Leonid Brezhnev, May 1968, confidential politburo
discussion)

'At first, the personality of Mikhail Gorbachev aroused
delight,' wrote KGB General Vladimir Medvedev,
Gorbachev's chief bodyguard, and before that, one of
Brezhnev's. The voluble new general secretary, the only
full politburo member at Brezhnev's death to have completed a full course of study at a major university, showed
himself to be a 'volcano of energy', added the bodyguard.
'He worked until 1.00, 2.00 a.m., and when various

documents were being prepared—and they were limitless, for congresses, plenums, meetings, and summits—he would go to bed after 3.00, and he always rose at 7.00 or 8.00."[1] Just the fact that Gorbachev showed up at his office, rather than work out of the hospital, signalled a profound change. No more walking corpses waving from atop a mausoleum!

Political power in the Soviet system was hyper-centralized, and dictated not only what people could see on television or learn at school, but also what the economy produced or did not produce. The general secretary, if he so desired, could initiate measures affecting the lives of 285 million people. But he could not implement new policies alone. Gorbachev selected Yegor Ligachev, eleven years his senior, to be the unofficial number two and run the nerve centre CC Secretariat. He brought the Levia-than economic ministries under his watch by promoting Nikolai Ryzhkov to replace Tikhonov as head of govern-ment. Foreign policy was taken from Gromyko (after twenty-eight years) and given to Georgian party chief Edu-ard Shevardnadze, a one-time police official whose lack of diplomatic experience ensured Gorbachev a free hand. Alexander Yakovlev, returned from a ten-year exile as ambassador to Canada, was made CC secretary for ideol-ogy (formally under Ligachev). This new inner circle, inherited from Andropov, continued to puzzle over the reformist generation dilemma: how to bridge the gap between socialism's ideals and its disappointing realities, within the context of the superpower competition.

Technically, party discipline made all officials beholden to party pronouncements, but to generate 'support' and pre-empt possible foot-dragging in the CC, state ministries, regions, and republics, Gorbachev appealed directly to rank-and-file party members, the intelligentsia, and working people, through a campaign for openness (glasnost) in public life. After several televised trips around the country and abroad that showcased the energetic new general secretary, strict efforts to combat alcoholism, a nuclear accident at the Chernobyl power plant that radiated millions of people, the freeing of the dissident physicist Andrei Sakharov from internal exile, the renewal of Jewish emigration, the shuffling of editors at key periodicals, and the appearance of a few previously banned films and novels, people began to see that the changes were serious. Andropov-style 'discipline' campaigns in factories, however, brought no positive results. A push for 'acceleration'—intensive growth in select industrial branches, rather than the usual extensive growth—also fell flat. In early 1987, Gorbachev placed economic reform on the agenda of successive politburo meetings.

Following the ill-conceived anti-alcohol campaign, which drove production underground (thereby draining state coffers of major tax revenue) and aroused public ire, much care went into the 1987–8 economic reforms. Prime Minister Ryzhkov's draft proposals, prepared by the planning bureaucracy, were criticized as too timid by politburo member Yakovlev, who cited the views of prominent academic economists. The general secretary, appearing to steer a middle course, shepherded through a series of far-reaching laws on enterprise 'autonomy', direct relations among firms, and small-scale service-sector 'cooperatives'. Top social scientists brought into the policy-making process had also singled out 'social activism' as the sine qua non of successful economic reform, and Gorbachev permitted the formation of 'unofficial' associations as well as the workplace election of managers. A democratized, re-energized Communist Party was supposed to lead the whole reform process. And facilitating overall success was a world campaign to transcend the superpower confrontation.

Soviet budget expenditures on the military, whose full details politburo member Gorbachev learned only after becoming general secretary, accounted for a stunning 20–30 per cent of GDP. Initially, he allocated *more* money to defence, and sanctioned an offensive to break the stalemate in the Afghanistan War. Some Soviet generals, whose top ranks Gorbachev had not appointed or changed, may have been tired of the war, but just as many were leery of disarmament talks with the US. Be that as it may, a good third of Gorbachev's memoir is taken up with his goading not of the Soviet military establishment but of President Ronald Reagan (and after 1988, George Bush) into accepting steep reductions in nuclear arsenals, to 'free up' resources for peaceful economic reconstruction and to attract Western investment. After the USSR had begun a phased withdrawal from Afghanistan in the autumn of 1986, arms negotiations still dragged on. Soon, however, international public opinion, and a shared desire for a place in history, led to a number of breakthrough agreements as well as promises of 'aid' and 'partnership'.

That, in a nutshell, was it—perestroika. Gorbachev initiated an imperial retreat, which was cast as a deepening of the USSR's long-standing 'peace' policy, and revolutionized the USSR's relationship with the West. He also began a serious, if difficult attempt to unblock the Soviet economy. And he secured the politburo's approval to open the system to scrutiny by the domestic and foreign media, goad the Communist Party to earn and better exercise its vanguard role, and invite social activism and associations outside the party. Thus did the occupant of Brezhnev's old office captivate the world and confound the experts. What went wrong?

Just about everything.

Economic halfway house

Frustration with the planned economy had been a topic of internal wrangling for decades. A confidential report in June 1965 by the Soviet economist Abel Aganbegyan—later a top Gorbachev adviser—pointed out that the Soviet growth rate was slowing, just as the US rate seemed stronger, and that key sectors for the Soviet standard of living (housing, agriculture, services, and retail trade) were especially backward. By way of explanation, Aganbegyan singled out the exorbitant resources devoted to the military and the extreme centralism of economic management. He further noted that the Central Statistical Administration did not have a single computer or any prospect of acquiring one. His report was not published—self-defeating hyper-secrecy had been another of Aganbegyan's culprits—but in September 1965 Prime Minister Aleksei Kosygin did launch a major economic reform. It was aimed at improving planning, by allowing greater flexibility for enterprises, and at redressing the imbalance between the military and consumers.

Predictably, ministries and parallel CC departments resisted ceding authority to enterprises, while the military baulked at sacrifices to increase consumer goods. Even without such resistance, a little flexibility proved useless, since managers wanting to cut costs were not allowed to dismiss workers. Nor could costs be factored into prices, since repercussions from raising prices frightened the leadership even more than unemployment. The Kosygin reforms failed even before the 1968 Prague events undercut the will for experimentation. Instead, the Kremlin decided in the 1970s to pursue the computerization of production and planning, and to import Western technology. To overcome a cold-war ban on technology transfers, the KGB set up foreign front companies and conducted remarkably successful industrial espionage, but few of their acquisitions paid off. Soviet factories proved unwilling or unable to introduce the new technologies, particularly information systems. By the 1980s the entire Soviet Union had just 200,000 microcomputers, leaving aside their quality, while the US already had 25 million, and that number was about to skyrocket. The very engine that had powered a peasant society to superpower status—the industrial planned economy—seemed increasingly to be exerting a severe drag.[2]

Consider the Soviet steel industry, which produced 160 million tons annually, far more than any other country.[3] By the 1980s, Soviet manufacturers used more than one million sizes and shapes of rolled steel. Since it was impossible to predict the proportions of each size or shape to be needed by each firm, the planners provided a range to producers. But since every plant's performance was measured by the weight of its output, a producer got more 'credit' for heavier strip. There was, however, a greater need for the thinner varieties. With no choice, firms took the thicker strip. Perhaps they could barter it on the vast internal black market among firms. If not, they would machine it down to the desired thickness. Perversely, the sheared-off metal counted in the Soviet GDP, even though it was discarded and made the production of finished goods more costly. Furthermore, although manufacturers were forced to shave off a significant portion of metal they received, Soviet machines, cars, and refrigerators were far heavier than Western counterparts. Durable-goods factories were also rewarded not for profits but for output tonnage. In short, the logic of the planned economy was devastatingly simple: quantity ruled. And by the late 1970s and early 1980s, after decades of extensive growth, even quantity was becoming a problem.

Gorbachev's 1987–8 economic reforms sought to address both the underlying logic and the recent negative trends. His programme introduced what by Soviet standards was unprecedented autonomy and 'profit-loss calculation' for large enterprises across the whole economy, as well as 'joint ventures' (a revival of Lenin's 1920s concession policy) to attract foreign capital. Gorbachev also sought to improve the outlook for consumers by legalizing service companies under the guise of 'cooperatives'. This bold strategy (by Soviet standards) combined and reworked the major economic reforms of Eastern Europe: the Yugoslav self-management system in industry and Hungary's private service sector. But, immediately, Soviet cooperatives suffered from a reputation for shadiness, and from criminal groups extorting 'protection' payments. In industry, Gorbachev, like Kosygin before him, found himself relying on a recalcitrant ministerial bureaucracy to implement an improbable decentralization that would entail a significant loss of ministerial authority. Also like Kosygin, Gorbachev stopped short of permitting real (market) prices for inputs and output, undermining the effects of whatever autonomy enterprises did manage to exercise. Going halfway towards the benefits of market criteria turned out to be no way.

Such recurring contradictions in the Sisyphean attempts to have the planned economy reform itself, without undoing planning or socialism, were compounded by miscalculations. In a blitz to re-equip obsolete manufacturing plants, while also trying to force them to increase output, huge investments were sunk into machine building and engineering industries. The funds were wasted. At the same time, after world oil prices had sharply dropped in 1986, and devastated hard-currency earnings, Soviet imports of consumer goods were curtailed without new investments in domestic light industry, thereby putting tremendous pressure on the standard of living, even as perestroika raised expectations. Also, the economy's most advanced sectors (defence), whose exports might have paid for purchasing consumer goods, were targeted for drastic downsizing. Worst of all, imperial retrenchment—Gorbachev's ace in the hole—*cost* money, to pay for decommissioning Soviet troops and arming former clients to defend themselves. Like the self-inflicted financial debacle that resulted from the anti-alcohol campaign, these blunders, the work of the country's top economists, were devastating.[4]

That a concerted, expert-advised reform had made matters worse came as a shock. Prior to 1985, the planned economy—greased with extensive black marketeering, choked by phenomenal waste, and increasingly dependent on key foreign imports—had stagnated, but it had functioned. Compared with their parents and grandparents, the Soviet population was better fed, better clothed, and better educated. Comparisons, however, were made not with the Soviet past, or developing countries, but with the richest nations in the world, and both the leadership and population expressed increasing impatience. *To compete with advanced capitalism* the only recourse seemed to be going beyond partial reforms and introducing the very mechanisms, private property and the market, whose suppression constituted the essence of socialism—in short, undoing the revolution and the regime's identity. Gorbachev, understandably, hesitated. But the relaxation of controls had created an economic halfway house. A desperate attempt at restoring fully centralized planning in 1990 proved utterly unworkable. Output plummeted. Shortages and queues became more severe than during wartime. The Soviet government solicited and received large Western loans, which were called 'aid' and earmarked to purchase Western goods, but many of the imports proved to be cast-offs, for which the country sank into deep foreign debt.[5]

Ideological self-destruction

Glasnost remained mostly a slogan right through 1986. Even geographical locations that *could* be indicated on Soviet maps were still being shown inaccurately, to foil foreign spies, as if satellite imaging had not been invented, while many cities were entirely missing (one could read about them in foreign publications). Widespread fictitious economic accounting was foiling planners to the point where the KGB employed its own spy satellites to ascertain the size of the Uzbek cotton harvest, but the spy agency itself suffered from internal falsifications. Clearly, some measure of openness was needed for the operation of the system, let alone for the people's dignity. This became very painfully clear in April 1986, when the world's worst nuclear catastrophe, at Chernobyl, demonstrated the depth of the Soviet Union's problems and the dangers as well as the increasing impossibility of hyper-secrecy. The radiation cloud, which made a mockery of the reflexive denials by Soviet officials, forced a tragic breakthrough.

In the autumn and winter of 1986–7, the Soviet media, with the general secretary's encouragement, set out to demonstrate an imperative for change by seizing upon issue after issue that had been taboo: the abortion epidemic, poverty, drug addiction, the Afghanistan War, Stalin-era deportations of entire nationalities. Long-banned films, plays, and books were unblocked, galvanizing the state-supported intelligentsia. Each step fanned speculation about how far it would go—would Solzhenitsyn's *Gulag Archipelago*, a literary indictment of the entire Soviet system, including Lenin, see the light of day? It did. That so much had been hidden and banned greatly magnified the reaction to each new offering in what was, after all, the official Communist Party media (non-state newssheets were started, but their circulation remained minuscule). The weekly newspaper *Arguments and Facts*, launched in the late 1970s, achieved a circulation above thirty million during perestroika—the most of any paper in the world—and its editors received 5,000 to 7,000 letters per day. The exhilaration—truth!—was widely and deeply felt.

By 1989, however, readers' letters bespoke the profound

disillusionment characteristic of defectors. 'What sort of a government is it [that] allows only selected people to live normal family lives?' wrote M.F., from the city of Kharkov. 'Why is it that people in authority have everything, flats, dachas, and money, and others have nothing? . . . I am a simple woman. I used to believe in our government. Now I no longer believe.' A teenager warned not to

let our young people go to capitalist countries. Why? I had the chance to go to the United States on an exchange basis. I used to be a true patriot of our country and I turned into something really horrible. I became a human being. I think; I have my own opinions; it's a nightmare. After what I saw in the USA, it's impossible to live here . . . I sympathize with Gorbachev, but deep in my heart I am no longer a Soviet citizen and I don't care what's going on in the USSR and I don't believe in anything in this country.[6]

To be disillusioned, of course, one has to have had illusions. Glasnost demonstrated that, before 1985, most Soviet inhabitants, despite limitless grievances, accepted many of the basic tenets of the system. No longer. Peoples' identities, all the sacrifices, were betrayed—right when expectations had been raised.

Glasnost turned into a tsunami of unflattering comparisons because of past censorship, the obsession with the capitalist world, and the intelligentsia's apocalyptic inclinations—it beat itself into hysteria with a competition to appear the 'most radical'. The smash Friday night television variety show, *Vzglyad* (*Viewpoint*), portrayed the

Soviet people as utterly destitute and exploited, while the West came across as paved with gold and unreservedly free. A print journalist who had written one of the fiercest anti-American diatribes prior to 1985 became the editor of the mass-circulation illustrated magazine *Ogonyok* (*Flame*), and promptly turned it into the most widely read source of investigative reporting and a billboard of exaggerated pro-Americanism.[7] Grisly new details about Communist repressions further undermined the allegiance to socialism, and raised moral dilemmas. Mass graves were described by the very policemen who had dug them. Prosecutors who had destroyed innocent people were still on the job or enjoyed comfortable retirements, while their victims were dead or suffered meagre pensions. Journalists who had hounded 'enemies' for anti-Soviet agitation now hastened to publish those views. All previous life was revealed as a lie.

Under Khrushchev, the 'revelations' had come to a generation of Stalinists, people who saw the formerly concealed information not as discrediting socialism but as discrediting Stalin, and inspiring them to a renewal of socialism, a return to its 'Leninist roots'. At least initially, that is how much of the Khrushchev generation interpreted Gorbachev's glasnost. Indeed, in economics and politics, many of the ideas that came forward had first been developed in the 1960s—as if Sleeping Beauty had awoken after a twenty-year nap.[8] But soon the same process that had targeted Stalin began desanctifying Lenin, meaning the Soviet system in toto. A tiny group calling itself the Democratic Union, one of the new 'informals' or civic associations that had arisen, invited arrest by declaring itself a political party, against the Communist monopoly, waving the red, white, and blue flag of the (pre-Bolshevik) February 1917 revolution, and demanding the restoration of private property and the 'bourgeois order'. Their appeals reached few people, but indicated the suicidal dynamic of openness for the system.

Whatever the cleavages among the children of Khrushchev's de-Stalinization, *their* children had come of age in a different time. Most people under the age of 30—one-quarter of the Soviet population—were simply not interested in reforming socialism. Glasnost afforded them unprecedented access to the commercial culture and 'values' of capitalism. Their alienation was captured in such derogatory slang for their parents and elders as *Sovok*, for *Sovetskii chelovek*—a Soviet person.[9] Ligachev, appalled by the comments of the youth shown on Soviet television, visited the station, and asked the programming executive whether he had found the featured adolescents in a jail.[10] But attitudes among youth, like the demands to abolish the Soviet system, preoccupied the top leadership far less than did battling with the public defences of Stalinism. 'We [*sic*] were too long under the illusion', Gorbachev later explained, 'that the problem was simply the difficulty of winning support for perestroika'.[11] But it was unclear what, besides denouncing Stalin, 'support' entailed. Worse, the common enemy, Stalinist socialism, obscured the chasm between those who denounced Stalin in the name of reforming socialism, and those who denounced him in the name of repudiating socialism.

National movements also emerged in connection with 'support for perestroika'. At first, they were narrow and tentative. But in February 1988, the inhabitants of Karabakh, a predominantly ethnic Armenian 'autonomous province' that Stalin had placed inside neighbouring Azerbaijan, interpreted Gorbachev's policies to signify the 'righting' of historical wrongs and called for 'reunification' with Armenia. Thousands of people, many carrying Gorbachev portraits, packed the central square of the Armenian capital in solidarity. The local authorities in Karabakh unilaterally declared themselves part of Armenia. Mass protests ensued in Azerbaijan in November 1988. Some Azerbaijanis in an ethnically mixed industrial town searched buses, hospitals, and apartment buildings for Armenians; thirty-one people were killed and hundreds wounded. Karabakh was placed under direct rule by Moscow, but tensions only escalated. Hundreds of thousands of people became refugees. The population of both countries was permanently mobilized, but not as Gorbachev had envisioned. Verbal condemnations of nationalists did nothing to stop them.

What were called 'popular fronts for the support of perestroika' also appeared in Lithuania, Latvia, and Estonia, and, with cross-border copying, in Ukraine and Belarus as well. Organized by the party and the KGB at Gorbachev's command, to outflank opponents of 'reform', the fronts brought together disparate groups,

1. Mikhail Gorbachev and Yegor Ligachev, visiting Prague, 1969, one year after the crackdown against the Prague Spring. The two provincial party chieftains learned first hand that the Soviet presence in Eastern Europe was widely opposed as an occupation regime.

2a. Leonid Brezhnev, bedecked with medals and propped up by his bodyguard, Vadim Medvedev (right), October 1979. The Soviet leader had just delivered a speech in East Germany, whose party boss, Erich Honecker (left), outlived Brezhnev, but was swept away in 1989, right before East Germany disappeared.

2b. KGB chief Yuri Andropov (in white hat), on a rest cure in his native Stavropol province, teaming up in dominoes with the local party host, Mikhail Gorbachev (in worker's cap), 1970s.

3. Brezhnev-era politburo, November 1980, whose only relative youth was Gorbachev (centre rear). Far right, Andrei Gromyko. Third from right, Yuri Andropov. Fourth from right, Nikolai Tikhonov. Centre, Brezhnev. Third from left, Mikhail Suslov. Second from left, Viktor Grishin. Konstantin Chernenko is obscured.

Артур Кальтбаум

ЗВЕЗДЫ
И
ФИЛЬМЫ

Wydawnictwa Artystyczne i Filmowe

4. Cover of *Stars and Films*, 1966, translated into Russian from Polish. Foreign films and Western mass culture invaded the Soviet bloc. Top row: Shirley MacLaine (US), Audrey Hepburn (US), Marcello Mastroaianni (Italy), Monica Vitti (Italy); middle row: Leslie Caron (France), Larisa Luzhina (Estonia), Jean-Claude Brialy (France), Jacqueline Sassard (France); bottom: Inna Gulaya (Ukraine), Brigitte Bardot (France).

5a. KGB delegation in Gdansk, Poland, 1979, site of mass strikes that led to the formation of Solidarity in 1980. Second from right, head of Soviet esponiage and later KGB chief Vladimir Kryuchkov. Third from right, Oleg Kalugin, who had worked in the Washington station and became the youngest person ever to reach general rank. Far right, Nikolai Leonov, who rose to become chief analyst.

5b. General Secretary Andropov, half dead upon taking over for Brezhnev, 1983.

6a. Chernobyl, 1986. The exploded reactor, history's worst nuclear accident, radiated millions of people, including flimsily clad emergency crews, but helped transform the slogan of glasnost (openness) into a reality. Russia and other post-Soviet states continue to operate reactors identical in design to the one at Chernobyl.

6b. The AvtoVAZ car factory purchased from Fiat in the 1960s, and more modern than the bulk of Soviet manufacturing. AvtoVAZ made more cars than any other factory in the world, but required thirty times more man-hours to produce a car than did a US or Japanese factory, to say nothing of quality. In the late 1980s and throughout the 1990s, AvtoVAZ was looted by management.

7. Mikhail Gorbachev, addressing the newly established Congress of People's Deputies, May 1989. The Congress shattered many taboos, not least of which was the fact that its proceedings were televised live.

8a. Suppression of a demonstration by the self-styled 'Democratic Union', Pushkin Square, Moscow, June 1989. Responding to glasnost by raising Russia's pre-Communist white, blue, and red flag and calling for restoration of the 'bourgeois order', the DU assembled fewer than a dozen protesters, who were hauled away in the mini-bus. Just over two years later, the tricolor would replace the hammer and sickle over the Kremlin.

8b. Yegor Ligachev, 1990. Ligachev commanded vast authority throughout the Soviet establishment, and eveyone, especially the press, expected him to wield that power and bring a halt to the reforms. But he never did.

including reformist party officials, and advocated first economic and then political 'sovereignty'—a term that seemed consonant with Gorbachev's emphasis on self-actualization. Undercover KGB operatives sought to keep these ever-growing movements within 'acceptable' bounds, but no one was sure what those bounds were, and events moved quickly. Street demonstrations in which some speakers, claiming to be supporting 'reform', demanded independence were broadcast on regional state television. Some leaders in the movements also came around to embracing demands for a multi-party political order and private property, both of which meant an end to the Soviet system.

There seemed to be no one ready to defend socialism and the Union, except those castigated as 'Stalinists' opposed to 'reform'! But the defenders of the system, in the CC and elsewhere, Gorbachev boxed in brilliantly, beating back their challenges at every party forum.

Virtuoso tactician

Gorbachev knew that far from all party officials shared his commitment to democratizing socialism, and, from the outset, he had been wary of an apparat revanche. Behind the scenes there was widespread foot-dragging, of course, but, at a February 1988 CC plenum, Yegor Ligachev, the number two official, openly argued for an end to glasnost's wholesale blackening of the Soviet past and, by implication, of the status quo. The mood in the hall was supportive of Ligachev and his call to rein in glasnost. The next month, as if in response, a firestorm broke over a Leningrad schoolteacher's letter to the editor of a rear-guard newspaper. Nina Andreeva's 'I Cannot Compromise Principles' attacked 'left-liberals', who 'falsify the history of socialism' and 'try to make us believe that the country's past was nothing but mistakes and crimes, keeping silent about the greatest achievements of the past and the present'.[12] The letter appeared in print the day Gorbachev left on a trip to Yugoslavia, and, as was party custom, his place was temporarily assumed by Ligachev. After Gorbachev's return, at the next politburo meeting, the general secretary casually brought the letter up, and, as pre-arranged, Alexander Yakovlev condemned it as an 'anti-perestroika manifesto'. Aspersions were cast on Ligachev and the Secretariat for overseeing the letter's publication.

Analysts at the time misperceived this important turn of events as evidence of determined apparat resistance rather than of Gorbachev manipulation. Gorbachev writes obliquely in his memoirs that the letter 'contained information known only to a relatively narrow circle'. Ligachev writes that Gorbachev had the circumstances of publication investigated and *privately* exonerated him of responsibility. Gorbachev never made a public disavowal of the suspicions. On the contrary, with the avid assistance of the Soviet and foreign media Ligachev was made into an unwitting instrument in the general secretary's efforts to cultivate society's sympathies and to pressure the apparat publicly to demonstrate that it was not anti-perestroika. Gorbachev also fashioned himself a scapegoat for economic failures: the Ligachev-led conservatives were strangling the reforms. To top it all off, he continued to enjoy Ligachev's loyalty, owing to party discipline and to the insincere private exculpation. 'Without knowing it,' Gorbachev writes with evident satisfaction, 'Nina Andreeva actually helped us'.[13] But his clever manipulation simply stirred up even greater popular fury at the party, without magically transforming the behaviour of apparatchiks, let alone the economy.

The general secretary expended extraordinary effort urging all levels of the apparat that *not* to take the risks of political reform would be even more dangerous. In 1987–8, he had managed to coax the politburo into agreeing to 'democratize' the party with competitive elections. Accustomed to lifetime appointments and perquisites in exchange for following orders, most party officials, even those who had reformist inclinations, did not know how to address a public reconfigured as voters. Nor did functionaries appreciate being held personally accountable for Stalin's crimes. The courageous types who heeded the call for the vanguard to lead 'perestroika' discovered that, in the absence of anticipated economic improvements, they were 'leading' little more than angry public ventilations over heretofore unmentionable problems, for which the party was being blamed. And, while party members among Moscow's intelligentsia were consumed in debates on history and freedom, wrote one *New York Times* reporter of a

July 1988 party conference, 'the delegates from the provinces want[ed] to talk about empty stores, dirty rivers, hospitals without water, and factories with deteriorating assembly lines'.[14]

Somehow, the Communist Party was supposed to be both the instrument and the object of perestroika, but, at that same July conference, Gorbachev, still seeking a reliable political base and levers of power, unveiled a plan to revive the soviets. Power had been seized in the names of the soviets in October 1917, yet these councils embodying a vision, like Jacobin clubs, of radical, direct democracy (rather than representative democracy) had long since atrophied. Now, local soviets were to be revived by means of contested elections, and these were to be accompanied by elections to a new all-union body, a Congress of People's Deputies, which would in turn choose representatives to a thoroughly revamped USSR Supreme Soviet, or working parliament. This plan, nominally only a refurbishment of existing institutions, meant moving beyond the party's hereditary power and acquiring a popular mandate—a test that the vast majority of sitting party officials who stood for election in early 1989 to the Congress failed miserably. Gorbachev exempted himself and the rest of the leadership from the competitive elections, but the new political situation was evident from the seating in the Congress hall: except for Gorbachev, politburo members sat not in the presidium, but in a gallery off to the side.

Reinvigoration of the soviets was accompanied by a

further, behind-the-scenes weakening of the party apparat's power. Acutely aware that the top echelon had turned on a previous reformer, Khrushchev, compelling his 'request to retire' in October 1964, and evidently not content with the results of his manipulation of the Nina Andreeva affair, Gorbachev went after Ligachev's power base. In September 1988, prior to the election campaign for the Congress of People's Deputies, he pulled off a 'reorganization' of the party Secretariat. Citing a need to improve the work of the CC, Gorbachev created a series of separate, labour-intensive party commissions, each headed by a politburo member. Suddenly, there was no time for collective Secretariat meetings, or for its Union-wide supervisory functions of the still intact Union-wide party committees, whether for coordinating the elections to the Congress or for a conspiracy against the general secretary. Thus, while still holding to his Leninist faith in the potential of the party mass, Gorbachev *deliberately* broke the might of the apparat fifteen months before he relented (February 1990) on the demands formally to abolish the Communist Party's monopoly. But, strange as it might seem, he failed to grasp that by undermining the party Secretariat and enhancing the state (the Supreme Soviets of the Union and of the republics) he was exchanging a unitary structure for a federalized one.

In the Russian empire of the tsars there had been no national republics, just non-ethnic provinces. National republics formed when the empire broke apart in the First World War, and, though the Red Army reconquered most of these territories, resistance by the new republics helped prevent their dissolution and absorption into Soviet Russia. Instead, an innovative compromise—the Union of Soviet Socialist Republics (USSR)—was reached in December 1922. Eventually, the Union came to have fifteen nationally designated republics, each with a state border, constitution, parliament, and (after 1944) a ministry of foreign affairs. In the similarly polyglot US, there were many Poles in Chicago but no Autonomous Polish Republic of Illinois—or Mexican Republic of California. Rather, the US was a single 'nation of nations' comprising fifty non-ethnic 'states' that were really provinces. The Soviet Union was a kind of 'empire of nations', since fifteen of its nations had statehood. To keep this nationally structured federation of states together, the Soviet leadership relied on the pyramid-like hierarchy of the Communist Party.

What was the Communist Party? It was not a political party in the Western sense, but a conspiracy to take power, which it did in 1917, after which a new revolutionary government was formed, and there were a few calls to abolish the party. Instead, the party found a role in power. That took place during the Civil War (1918–21), when the former Russian empire territories were reconquered, tsarist officers were recruited to the Red Army, and 'political commissars' were introduced alongside the military experts to guarantee their loyalty. Such, haphazardly, became the model for the whole country: in every institution, from schools to ministries, party members, or commissars, were called upon to act as guarantors of loyalty and correct politics. But soon Soviet army officers, bureaucrats, teachers, and engineers ceased to be holdovers from the tsarist period. The country trained its own 'Red', or party-member, experts, yet the separate party organizations shadowing the experts were not removed. On the contrary, the bureaucracy of the party continued to grow alongside the bureaucracy of the state, and both performed essentially the same functions: management of society and the economy. Thus, the Soviet Union acquired two parallel, overlapping administrative structures: party and state. Of course, if the redundant party were removed, one would be left not just with the Soviet central state bureaucracy, but also with a voluntary association of national republics, each of which could legally choose to withdraw from the Union. In sum, the Communist Party, administratively redundant to the Soviet state and yet critical to its integrity, was like a bomb inside the core of the Union.

In this light, the proposals immediately after Stalin's death made by Lavrenti Beria stand out as a potentially fateful moment. A supremely skilled and murderous organizer, Beria was the kingpin of the state's military-industrial complex, which beginning with the 1930s industrialization and continuing through the Second World War and the onset of the cold war, had got the upper hand over the party apparat in the dualist party–state system. In 1953, Beria proposed eliminating the administrative role of the party in favour of the state and enhancing the position of native elites in the Union republics (his other power base). Whether these proposals would have better secured the Soviet Union's nationally federalized, party-dependent integrity will never be known.[15] The rest of the Soviet leaders pounced on Beria before he pounced on them. Nikita Khrushchev, with the backing of the apparatchiks whom the technocratic Beria disdained, won the ensuing power struggle. Khrushchev deepened the re-assertion (launched in 1952 at the 19th Party Congress) of the party's role vis-à-vis the state.

But the party apparat that Khrushchev reinvigorated soon turned against him. Thus, the Soviet party–state seemed both to call forth efforts at socialist renewal and to block those efforts. This reformist/conservative dialectic was the political dynamic that had produced Gorbachev, and that he had set out to master, first with the Nina Andreeva manipulation of Ligachev, and then with the 'reorgnization' manœuvre against the party Secretariat. But that momentous act set off a bomb inside the Union structure that undercut all his clever tactics.[16] The most poignant moment of Gorbachev's memoir, written years after the fact, comes when he writes of the 1988–9 political reforms that he failed at that time 'to put forward a real program' for 'the transformation of the unitary state into a federal state'.[17] But, by sabotaging the party Secretariat, this is exactly what he did, unawares. As his top military adviser Sergei Akhromeev wrote in 1991, 'higher republic organs of power, in line with the USSR Constitution, were not subordinated to equivalent USSR organs.

They were connected only by the influence of the party and party discipline. ... Did the politburo headed by Gorbachev understand all this? They should have.'[18]

Even had he not (owing to his perception of reform/conservative dynamics) waylaid the Secretariat, Gorbachev would have had his hands full bringing to heel the Soviet Union's fifteen Union republics, because they had clearly defined state borders and their own state institutions. Now, with the party's central control mechanism shattered and its ideology discredited, and the tentacles of the planned economy disrupted, Gorbachev discovered that the Supreme Soviets of the republics began to act in accordance with what he had unintentionally made them: namely, parliaments of *de facto* independent states. In March 1990—the fifth anniversary of his ascension to power—he manœuvred the politburo into authorizing, and the USSR Supreme Soviet into voting, an executive presidency for him. But central power had been dispersed, and the survival of the Union was in doubt.

The missing Suslov

Gorbachev's assault on the conservatives' potential power base, meanwhile, succeeded spectacularly. But it was completely unnecessary. Ligachev moans in his memoirs that for a long time he *missed* the significance of the Secretariat's 1988 'reorganization'. Even after belatedly seeing through Gorbachev's camouflage, Ligachev shrank from raising the matter at subsequent politburo meetings. When someone else brought it up, Gorbachev pointedly asked Ligachev if he personally needed a Secretariat. The party's number two official confesses he remained silent, for fear of showing ambition, shuffled back to his office, and began writing alarmist letters to his boss. 'The bitter truth', Ligachev remonstrates, 'is I turned out to be right'. But, if Ligachev had known *back then* that socialism and the Union were in danger, the bitter truth is that the person best positioned to do whatever was necessary to stop the general secretary lacked the wits and the stomach to do so. Ligachev had taken over the office once occupied by Mikhail Suslov, who had helped mastermind Khrushchev's removal. But he was no Suslov. Passing Ligachev's letters to the archives, Gorbachev continued on the haphazard quest for reformed socialism. Only it was not reform. It was dissolution.

Because he shared Gorbachev's belief in the possibility of energizing the system, Ligachev refuses to accept that perestroika is precisely what precipitated the system's demise, or even that the blame lay with the man he had helped put in power. Instead, Ligachev rails against the hijacking of perestroika by 'radical conspirators', such as Alexander Yakovlev, intent on destroying socialism. 'The real drama of perestroika', writes Ligachev, 'was that the process ... was distorted'.[19] Here we have the inept counterpart to Gorbachev's brilliant scapegoating of the conservatives. True, Yakovlev constantly outmanoeuvred Ligachev (when, for example, the politburo decided to reprimand someone in the media, Yakovlev 'deferred' to his nominal boss, Ligachev, reserving for himself the role of affording encouragement behind the scenes). But Ligachev's endorsement of Yakovlev's self-promotion as the 'father of perestroika' fails to do the general secretary justice. The decisive 'conspirator' was the general secretary.[20] More to the point, like a souvenir Matroshka doll, inside Gorbachev there was Khrushchev; inside Khrushchev was Stalin, and inside him, Lenin. Gorbachev's predecessors had created an edifice lined with hidden booby traps that provoked their own detonation by calling forth the reformist impulse.

Having deliberately crippled the centralized party machine, Gorbachev retained control over the executive pillars of the Soviet state: the KGB and interior ministry (MVD), whose 'republic' branches were totally subordinated to Moscow, and the unified Soviet army. Yet, although the gargantuan KGB collected voluminous information, glasnost removed people's fears and neutralized its capacity to intimidate.[21] The difficulties of using the army domestically were made plain in April 1989, when a few hundred demonstrators in the Georgian capital, some advocating independence, were violently dispersed, resulting in around twenty deaths, an incident that threatened to ignite the entire Georgian nation. As everyday political instruments, the KGB, the MVD, and the army were no substitute for the party. Their use, moreover, was now subject to debate in the revamped Soviet parliament as well as in the republic legislatures.

Still, had troops been used *swiftly and massively*, as Machiavelli might have advised, to enforce the priority of USSR laws in 1989 or even 1990, they could have set back independence movements and bought time. That was precisely what took place in January 1990 in Azerbaijan, where the secession of the Armenian enclave Karabakh had helped bring the nationalist-minded Azerbaijan 'national front' to power. On the pretext of stopping anti-Armenian pogroms, which had ended six days before, 17,000 Soviet troops swooped in, arrested a few leaders of the front, and restored the rule of Communist officials more pliant to Moscow, at a cost of around 200 lives and much popular resentment. The other republics, cognizant of such a possible use of force, endeavoured to split off MVD, KGB, and army officers stationed on their territories, achieving only limited success. Their greater ally was Gorbachev. The Soviet leader's commitment to humane socialism, which had led him to destabilize the system, also made him hesitate to restabilize it. Even in Azerbaijan, Gorbachev refused to suppress the national front ruthlessly, instead inviting many of its members into the new government, thereby negating many of the effects of the forceful action.[22]

For decades, Eastern Europe's experience had shown that, in the teeth of the competition with capitalism, efforts to reform planning (without relinquishing socialism's commitment against the 'exploitation' inherent in private property) failed and unsettled the whole system. This was even truer of the efforts to combine wider latitude for the press or civic associations with the Communist Party's monopoly. What, after all, had necessitated sending tanks to Budapest and Prague? One would think that the more recent lessons (1980–1) of Poland's Solidarity would have raised even more profound questions. Yet to Gorbachev, and indeed to most analysts, the main drama of reform involved not squaring the circle, but a struggle between reformers and conservatives. The conservative 'resistance' during perestroika, however, was inept, while Gorbachev's 'sabotage' of the system, though largely inadvertent, was masterly. Thus, the 'real drama of reform', obscured by fixation on the conservatives, featured a virtuoso tactician's unwitting, yet extraordinarily deft, dismantling of the Soviet system—from the planned economy, to the ideological legitimacy for socialism, to the Union.

Well into 1990, as calls for an overthrow of the regime multiplied and republic legislatures passed laws superseding those of the USSR, Gorbachev continued to state publicly that the principal obstacle to 'reform' was opposition by 'conservatives'. This was *after* Eastern Europe had imploded.

4

Waiting for the end of the world

There are some things—I call them last stands—that
must be defended to the death, as in the battles for
Moscow [1941] and Stalingrad [1942–3]. It is
impossible to split us apart. We cannot be split apart,
comrades. There will be a terrible war, there will be
clashes.

> (Mikhail Gorbachev, 28 November 1990)

The Soviet Union resembled a chocolate bar: it was
creased with the furrowed lines of future division, as
if for the convenience of its consumers.

> (Nikolai Leonov, Chief Analyst of the KGB)

Eastern Europe was the weak link. In 1980–1, during Solidarity, the Soviet politburo pressured the Polish leadership to crack down, but internally Moscow recognized that
its ability to implement the so-called Brezhnev Doctrine—
the use of force to maintain loyal socialist regimes in Eastern Europe—was exhausted.[1] At Chernenko's funeral in
1985, Gorbachev advised East European leaders that they

were on their own.[2] Thereafter, he began to make this momentous fact public. In 1986–7, the Soviet military, preparing for all contingencies, studied what they would do should the Warsaw Pact suffer major difficulties. The high command opposed imperial retreat, except perhaps to 'cede' East Germany in exchange for a neutral unified Germany, thereby weakening NATO. The cost of having acquired a position in Europe in the Second World War, and maintained it through armed interventions, made the stakes very high. Above all, no one could be sure how changes in Eastern Europe might reverberate within the Soviet Union.

Appointing the neophyte Eduard Shevardnadze to replace the veteran Gromyko as foreign minister attested to the importance Gorbachev attached to foreign policy.[3] Now unencumbered, the Soviet leader deliberately neglected the satellites, aside from mostly indirect prodding of Eastern Europe's anti-reform leaders. This distancing, together with the exit from Afghanistan, formed part of a strategy to defuse the superpower confrontation, thereby reducing the strain on his country and raising his own profile. It worked like a charm. Gorbachev achieved major, albeit asymmetrical arms reduction and a deep détente with an American president who in 1983 had vilified the Soviet Union as the 'evil empire'. Perestroika-like 'reforms' were underway in Poland and Hungary, and, though hardliners held out in East Germany and Romania, Western Europe was delirious with 'Gorbymania'. For four years, he strut the world stage like a grand statesman transforming the international system, imagining his country would soon be accepted as part of the West.

Then, the floor caved in. In reformist Poland, the Solidarity opposition, driven underground in late 1981, returned stronger than ever, and, in the June 1989 elections, it won 99 of the 100 seats it was allowed to contest. Even though the Polish Communists had rigged matters to guarantee themselves a parliamentary majority, General Jaruzelski—who had ordered the 1981 crackdown— invited the anti-Communist opposition to form the government. Reform had led to regime capitulation. In un-reforming East Germany, the results were the same. Tens of thousands of people fled westwards by obtaining tourist visas to neighbouring socialist countries and then applying for asylum at Western embassies. The flow increased in September 1989 after Hungary, prompted by West German credits, removed the barbed wire at its border with Austria. With popular (and Soviet) pressure mounting against the East German regime, someone in the GDR leadership, at a bungled press conference on 9 November, accidentally declared foreign travel open. Crowds began dismantling the Berlin wall!

No one could figure out what the enormous Soviet military establishment was up to. It turns out that they were mostly kept out of the policy loop. Before 1989, according to Marshall Sergei Akhromeev, Gorbachev never once discussed scenarios for Eastern Europe with the Soviet military. In March 1990, the brass blew their fuse, denouncing Gorbachev's surrogate, Shevardnadze, for having failed to consult them—at a meeting the foreign minister failed to attend. Of course, Gorbachev had never planned to 'lose' the bloc. Overtaken by events, he began pressing for guarantees that NATO would not absorb East Germany or expand eastwards. But, in May 1990, US President George Bush pressed the issue of German unification *within* NATO. Two months later, Gorbachev presented the more cautious West German Chancellor Helmut Kohl with the gift of a phased, complete withdrawal of Soviet troops, without trying to secure German neutrality.[4] Nor could the Soviet leader save the Warsaw Pact. A foreign policy aimed at a 'common European home' had led to the Soviet Union's ejection from Europe. 'I would be less than sincere,' Gorbachev wrote, 'if I said that I had foreseen the course of events and the problems that the German question would eventually create'.[5]

The Soviet leader's dramatic non-intervention to retain Eastern Europe should be viewed in the light not only of the USSR's 1981 *de facto* internal repeal of the Brezhnev doctrine, but also of France's long, futile war to hold Algeria or the brutal tenacity of the Dutch and Portuguese throughout Asia and Africa. Domestically, the Soviet leader's aides pitched the 'sacrifice' of Eastern Europe as essential for improving relations with the West, which they argued was itself an imperative, since the USSR could no longer afford the superpower competition.[6] But for the Soviet military and security establishment, now burdened with the logistics of a hurried, humiliating retreat, Gorbachev's 'transformation' of the international system meant the surrender of all the gains of the Second World War. Eastern Europe's exit from the Soviet orbit had an equally dramatic impact on the Soviet republics, which Gorbachev had unbound from the Communist Party and planned economy centralism, and placed within the vortex of electoral politics.

In March 1990 the parliament of Lithuania voted to secede from the Union, 124 to 0 (with 9 abstentions). The Estonian and Latvian parliaments declared 'transitional periods' to independence. Though tiny, the three Baltic republics, which had been independent between 1918 and 1940, seemed to present a special challenge. But in June 1990 the *Russian* republic declared its 'sovereignty'—vis-à-vis *Moscow*—asserting the primacy of republic laws over Union ones. The parliaments of Ukraine, Belorussia, and newly renamed Moldova (Moldavia) followed Russia's lead to declarations of sovereignty. Armenia, radicalized by Karabakh, followed Lithuania, declaring independence. Suddenly, Gorbachev announced plans for a new 'Union Treaty', to replace the 1922 original. Also, having previously managed to appear a political centrist indispensable to all, he now openly joined forces with the 'left' to prepare a 500-day programme for a transition to the market. A few months later, however, in mid-September 1990, he just as suddenly renounced the 500-day plan and confederation plans, asked the Soviet parliament for special 'emergency powers', and began to add several proponents of 'order' to his government.

Accompanying Gorbachev's autumn 1990 lurch to the

'right', the first draft of a new Union Treaty was published. It accorded republics only limited control over enterprises and resources on their territories, maintained the primacy of Union laws, specified Russian as the state language, and failed to mention the USSR constitution's guarantee of secession. The draft may have appeased a disgruntled military and KGB, but it had no prayer of winning republic approval. Estonia, Latvia, and Lithuania had refused to take part in any discussions about a Union even before the draft's publication. The KGB publicly warned that the Union republics were following 'an East Germany scenario'. In January 1991 a contingent of special forces commenced a police operation in Lithuania, resulting in thirteen deaths, but the troops were quickly called off. The Soviet president, though commander in chief, disclaimed any involvement and failed to discipline anyone. Armenia, Georgia, and Moldova announced they also would have nothing to do with the Union. In March 1991 a new draft of a Union Treaty restored the right to secession (piled with restrictions), but many republics did not bother to respond. The next month, Gorbachev abruptly reversed course once more, tacking back to the 'left' and opening direct negotiations with the nine republics still willing to consider a relationship with Moscow. But he also kept the pro-unitary-state Soviet government in place.

Left, right, then left *and* right—the zigs and zags from mid-1990 into mid-1991 were hard to read. Back in December 1990, when a journalist asked whether he was moving to the right, Gorbachev had quipped, 'actually,

I'm going round in circles'.[7] Indeed, hardline critics mocked him as 'someone who has missed his train and is scurrying around the empty platform'.[8] But, despite the non-intervention in Eastern Europe, and Gorbachev's award of the Nobel Peace Prize in October 1990, no one could exclude the possibility of an attempted crackdown to save the Union. That remained true even after April 1991, when Gorbachev placed his hopes in negotiations with the republics, above all Russia—meaning his *bête noire*, Boris Yeltsin. Would Yeltsin compromise to salvage some form of a Union, and if so, would it matter? Would Gorbachev or perhaps others in the Soviet establishment use massive force to hold off dissolution, or to make others pay for the country's humiliation? The decolonization of Western Europe's *overseas* possessions had been drawn out and bloody. The Soviet land empire, with several million well-armed troops and a vast doomsday arsenal, could have unleashed a far nastier bloodbath, even an end to the world.

The crowd-bather

Born in 1931, the same year as Gorbachev, to a peasant family in a village east of the Ural Mountains, Boris Yeltsin was almost drowned by a drunken priest in a baptism bath. During the Second World War, far from the front, the teenage Boris disassembled a grenade to see what was inside, losing two fingers. He almost died of typhus exploring a swampy forest, and requested the floor at his school graduation to deliver a peroration of the collective resentments against an abusive teacher, for which his continuation in higher education was blocked, despite good grades. But Yeltsin took his case to higher authorities, and won, eventually gaining entrance to the Urals Polytechnic University. In 1955—while Gorbachev was writing a senior thesis on the superiority of socialism over capitalism—Yeltsin wrote his on the construction of coal mines. He entered the party in 1961 (nine years later than Gorbachev), and in 1968 was shifted from the building trusts to the provincial party apparat. In 1976 Yeltsin became party boss of his native Sverdlovsk, a strategic territory that produced tanks, aircraft, and nuclear and biological weapons.

As a provincial first secretary, Yeltsin excelled at what one biographer aptly calls the 'bain de foule' (bathing in the crowd). He rode mass transit conspicuously, appeared live on local television, and met blue-collar workers and students, answering written questions for hours. His 'favourite routine', writes the biographer, 'was to glance at a slip of paper calling for the dismissal of an especially incompetent or corrupt official, and then announce, to loud applause: "Already fired. Next question."'[9] Such ham-handed populism came naturally to Yeltsin, and he had some economic results to back up the theatrics. Yegor Ligachev, in charge of personnel in Andropov's Kremlin, visited Yeltsin's fief for an unusually long four-day inspection in 1984. In 1985, after Gorbachev's elevation, Yeltsin was brought to Moscow as CC Secretary for Construction. Several months later he was named boss of the Moscow party committee, replacing Viktor Grishin, Gorbachev's erstwhile rival. Grishin's career was already finished. The crowd-bather would emerge as a new rival.

Sverdlovsk was a weightier bailiwick than Ligachev's Tomsk or Gorbachev's Stavropol, yet Yeltsin got to Moscow later than his provincial peers, and chafed as their subordinate.[10] He also found the capital tough going. His attacks on elite perquisites, and his imperious treatment of subordinates, made him anathema to the powerful party machine. In the autumn of 1987, Yeltsin clashed with Ligachev over apparatchik 'privileges', and then with Gorbachev, rising at a party gathering to accuse the general secretary of fostering sycophantism and being indecisive. Offering to resign, Yeltsin was bounced from the politburo and the leadership of the Moscow city party, though Gorbachev threw him a line, the post of deputy head of the construction industry, which Yeltsin took. Two years later, Gorbachev provided an even bigger gift when he introduced competitive elections for a new Congress of People's Deputies. Yeltsin resumed baiting unpopular apparatchiks like Ligachev—and they obliged, forming a commission to investigate whether his highly popular views were compatible with the party line. Running in the Moscow district, Yeltsin won election to the 1989 Congress in a 90 per cent landslide.

The two-week Congress riveted the country—its televised eight-hour sessions, during the workday, were seen by an estimated 200 million people—and Yeltsin attracted an enormous following inside and outside the hall as the unofficial leader of the 'democrats'. The KGB conducted an international smear campaign against him, and tapped his telephones (materials later discovered in a safe with annotations in Gorbachev's hand), but the surveillance did not stop Yeltsin. Fears of a KGB assassination also gripped Yeltsin's entourage. One night in October 1989, he did show up wet and bleeding at a police station, claiming to have been thrown off a bridge. The bridge was so high and the water so shallow that no one could have survived such a fall. Yeltsin's bodyguard and bathhouse confidant, Alexander Korzhakov, who arrived to clean the bleeding body with moonshine, has written that a depressed Yeltsin attempted suicide.[11] Rebounding, the crowd-bather was popularly elected in March 1990 to a Russian republic Congress of People's Deputies, and in May was elected by the Congress as chairman of its Supreme Soviet—by a four-vote margin.

Leading Russia's drive for 'sovereignty', Yeltsin, too, was a product of the Soviet system. But, whereas Ligachev favoured the Andropov school (tough discipline, suspicion of the West), and Gorbachev chased romantic ideals (party democracy, Western partnership), Yeltsin inclined towards paternalistic identification with 'the folk'. Wielding the common touch Gorbachev lacked, he promised 'radical reform', including a market economy, about which he knew nothing but which he and his supporters imagined would provide the better life and social justice that had been the promise of socialism.[12] On the new playing field of electoral politics Gorbachev had created, Yeltsin the martyred 'man of the people' presented a far greater challenge than had Ligachev, the 'conservative apparatchik' in the red-carpeted hallways. Not one to give up, Gorbachev reached into his bag of tactics and pulled out a referendum, to be held in March 1991, on preservation of the Union. Unable to block the vote, Yeltsin managed to attach a second question on creating a presidency for the Russian republic. With an 80 per cent turnout, three-quarters of the electorate supported a 'renewed Union'. True, six republics had not allowed the ballot on their territories, but the Soviet president had his 'mandate'. At the same time, however, Yeltsin launched a Union-challenging presidential election campaign, which he won resoundingly in June 1991.

Moscow now had two presidents, one elected by parliament (Gorbachev) and one (Yeltsin) by the people. That was the background to the Union Treaty negotiations between the leaders of nine republics and 'the centre' that opened in late April 1991. The working text dropped the word 'socialist', devolved most ministerial functions to the republics, upheld the supremacy of republic laws, called for the dissolution of the USSR Supreme Soviet, and made clear that Union membership was voluntary. This was worse than the deal on confederation that Gorbachev had rejected nine months previously in the 500-day plan. In late July 1991 an agreement was reached 'in principle'. Gorbachev went on television to praise the accord—

without divulging its contents—and then left on 4 August for vacation in the Crimea. The Treaty was to be signed in Moscow on 20 August. Confident in the support of the Kazakh leader Nursultan Nazarbaev, the Soviet president claims he remained concerned about Yeltsin's possible abandonment of the settlement. But Leonid Kravchuk of Ukraine did not even attend the negotiations.[13]

Two days before the signing ceremony, on 18 August in the early evening, a group of top Soviet officials arrived unsummoned at Gorbachev's Crimean dacha with a proposal for him to declare martial law. He refused. He also refused to resign outright or claim illness and resign temporarily in favour of his vice-president, Yanaev, returning 'healthy' when the dust settled. Rebuffed, the heads of the KGB, army, police, military-industrial complex, and civilian Soviet government went forward with the 'illness' scenario anyway. The demise of a unitary state had been made plain by the text of the Union Treaty, which, hoping to cause an uproar, they had leaked to *Moscow News* on 14 August (and which was republished in other papers the next day). The demise was also clear from Yeltsin's imperious decrees asserting the Russian republic takeover of the valuable USSR oil and natural gas industries on Russian territory, as well as his proclamations on forming a Russian republic KGB and a Russian defence ministry. If members of the Soviet government needed further incentive to act, the KGB chief exhibited the transcript of an eavesdropped conversation on 29–30 July among Gorbachev, Yeltsin, and Nazarbaev that named every top USSR official for removal.[14] On 19 August, the men who had stood by as Eastern Europe broke away, sent tanks rolling into Moscow.

Beer hall putsch

Even after becoming general secretary, Gorbachev—who had never served in the army—had remained wary of the Soviet military and the KGB. Using the pretext of the embarrassing May 1987 landing right behind Red Square of a small Cessna aeroplane flown from Germany by a teenager, he cleaned house, thoroughly purging the senior army ranks, and promoting the obscure Dmitry Yazov to defence minister. In 1988, when Gorbachev disarmed Yegor Ligachev by sabotaging the Secretariat, he transferred into that emasculated body KGB chief Chebrikov, who had been making public noises about the downside of reform. The new KGB chief, Vladimir Kryuchkov, later wrote that, at the time, he saw Gorbachev, the man responsible for fulfilling his lifelong ambition to head the KGB, as a hard-working leader who deserved full support.[15] In August 1991, however, Kryuchkov, pulling along Yazov, confined Gorbachev at the Crimean dacha and led a group that invoked the 'emergency powers' parliament had some time before granted the Soviet president.

Announcing its existence on 19 August 1991, the State Emergency Committee claimed eight members, after some had asked that their names be kept off decrees. Their stated goals were to uphold the laws and integrity of the Union, restore labour discipline, cut prices, and allocate money to schools, hospitals, and pensioners. They got expressions of 'support' from many provincial officials around Russia (and marginal extremists in Moscow). They sent out instructions to local branches of the KGB and interior ministry to fight a war on crime. They instituted a naval blockade of the Baltic republics, and moved armoured troops into Leningrad—a bastion of 'democrats'—as well as into Moscow. But the Committee also took pains to appear to adhere to the Soviet constitution. It was nominally headed by the next in line of succession—Vice-President Yanaev—though some had hoped the lead would go to the supposedly more resolute prime minister, Valentin Pavlov. After signing on as the country's new leader, Yanaev went home to drink. Pavlov also took to drinking, and then summoned medical assistance.[16]

Troop deployments were poorly coordinated among the various ministries involved, but also timid. The chief of Soviet ground forces flew to Ukraine, where there were 700,000 Soviet troops and officers sworn to loyalty to the high command in Moscow. The general suggested introducing martial law in the Ukrainian republic, the prerogative of republican legislatures, but the chairman of the Ukrainian parliament said it was not necessary, and the commander simply departed for Moscow.[17] Russian President Yeltsin managed to fly from Kazakhstan the morning of the putsch (19 August), land at the main government airport in Moscow, drive to his dacha, and then—although KGB troops had surrounded his dacha—ride from there with a small guard to the 'White House', site of the Russian republic government. At this richly symbolic site, the Russian leader rallied a core of defiant officials and civilians, and issued decrees that countermanded those of the putschists. Crack commandos positioned outside the Russian White House never received a firm order to storm the lightly guarded building. Their officers entered into contact with Yeltsin.[18]

Perhaps nothing did more to undermine the 'gang of eight' than the fact that they organized a televised press conference—and submitted to unscripted questions. Yanaev fumbled and appeared to be drunk. Not only Pavlov, but Yazov and Kryuchkov were absent. Failing to use the state media effectively, the Committee also allowed Western TV journalists to operate freely. At Soviet television, some staff defiantly showed footage of the street resistance in Moscow and Leningrad, letting the whole country see what the various layers of the KGB, military establishment, ministries, and party machine already knew from CNN. Not even key telephones were cut off. From inside the Russian White House, the 'chief' of Yeltsin's newly created Russian republic KGB 'was on the telephone nonstop, talking with commanders in the Moscow military district, with MVD forces, with KGB units', according to one eyewitness. 'He was telling everyone roughly the same thing: I'm calling at Yeltsin's behest, don't get tangled up in this business, keep your men and materiel out of it.' The general whom Yeltsin appointed as the Russian republic 'defence minister' did the same.[19]

One Russian commentator has noted that 'the second echelon of power stood aside'.[20] So did most of the first, despite their sympathies with the goal of saving the Union. Nikolai Leonov, the KGB's chief analyst, writes that 'among the senior generals there was ... disquiet, indecisiveness, disorder', adding that he knew the putsch was doomed the minute he saw its televised press conference.[21] Another high-ranking KGB official remarked bitterly: 'cowardly geezers who were good for nothing got together, and I fell in with them like a chicken into the plucker.'[22] The Committee's secret list of individuals to be incarcerated counted seventy names, mostly the high-profile 'democrats' whom the putschists despised. In the event, just five people were taken into custody.[23] (About 5,000 arrests had been carried out in *one night* of the Polish regime's 1981 crackdown against Solidarity.) For those inclined to emphasize the 'ruthlessness' of the plotters, consider that Yanaev had been using Beria's old Kremlin office, and Pavlov had been using Stalin's.

As late as Sunday 18 August, Defence Minister Yazov, when asked by the conspirators about the next step, had exploded, 'We have absolutely no plan.' Kryuchkov is said to have interjected, 'What are you saying, we have a plan.' Yet Yazov recalled that, 'I knew that we had no plan, aside from the elementary talking points that had been read aloud ... on Saturday.'[24] Twice the 68-year-old Yazov had been wounded at the meat-grinder front against the Nazis. His first wife had died of cancer; his second was crippled by a car accident in May 1991. By that time, Yazov had served more than five decades in the Soviet Armed Forces, only to watch Eastern Europe slip away and the Union unravel. On 19 August the nuclear suitcase with the codes for launching the Soviet doomsday arsenal was removed from Gorbachev and brought to the defence ministry, which already had the companion suitcase. Despondency or rage could have led Yazov and the General Staff to push some pretty large buttons.[25] Instead, early on 21 August, Yazov convened the high command and they collectively ordered all troops back to the barracks.

Undone, the putschists decided to fly to the Crimea and seek an audience with the one important person they had detained though not harmed—Gorbachev. Even the instigator of the plot, Kryuchkov, chose not to seek asylum in a friendly country but to join the group on its supplication flight. The veteran KGB general had been deeply involved in the bloody crackdown in Hungary in 1956 and the decade-long slaughterhouse of Afghanistan. But he had always been a deputy. In the wee small hours of 22 August, he was brought back from the Crimea on the Soviet president's plane, and arrested in Moscow by Russian republic officials. From prison, Kryuchkov begged for an audience with Gorbachev, writing, 'Mikhail Sergeevich! What an enormous feeling of shame—heavy, crushing, relentless, it's a permanent torment. When you were incommuni-

cado, I thought, how rough for you, for Raisa Maksi-
movna, the family, and I came to horror, despair.'[26]

At a press conference following his return to Moscow,
Gorbachev thanked the Russian president for securing his
release and, to the astonishment of everyone, defended
the Communist Party. Yeltsin soon publicly embarrassed
him with evidence of the party's complicity in the putsch,
and decreed an end to the party's existence. Because the
Soviet parliament had failed to return from summer
recess and condemn the putsch, the Soviet president saw
no alternative but to force it to disband. Witch-hunts and
demoralization paralysed the Soviet executive branch,
including the KGB and the defence ministry, where
'bedlam' prevailed.[27] Gorbachev, with Yeltsin's prodding,
recognized the independence of Lithuania, Latvia, and
Estonia. The putsch, rather than save the Union, radically
accelerated its demise.

National trees in the Union landslide

Street resistance to the putsch was greatest in Leningrad,
but it was Yeltsin's mounting of a hostile tank in Moscow to
address a crowd of resisters and news cameras that gave
rise to the comforting myth of the triumph of 'democrats'
over Communists. This is a partial truth concealing a
much larger one. Well before the putsch, press freedom
and competitive elections had become regular features
of political life. The Communist Party's monopoly had

ended, and the move to the market was willy-nilly underway. Of course, Gorbachev resisted a full embrace of the
market and stubbornly clung to the Communist Party.[28]
But those who condemn the Soviet leader for his
reluctance to let go forget that a critical aspect of his
commitment to reformed socialism was hesitation to
employ the full force of the USSR's repressive-military
machine. Gorbachev's move to the right in November
1990 resulted from his own disorientation as well as KGB
and military pressures. Yet his temporizing, including his
repeated instructions for these groups to prepare plans
for martial law,[29] paralysed them until the summer of
1991, by which time the Russian republic, and a Russian
president, had become authoritative sources of allegiance
for the central Soviet elite.

Initially, Yeltsin had played the Russian card against
Gorbachev without intending to break up the Union. So
did the Communist Party conservatives who formed a
Russian republic Communist Party in June 1990. These
opponents of Yeltsin supported Russia's declaration of
sovereignty, which passed overwhelmingly, as a way to
undermine Gorbachev, and in their minds, to save the
Union. Even Yeltsin's drive to create a Russian presidency
in 1991 envisioned using the new office not to displace
the Soviet president but to force Gorbachev to follow
his lead. Of course, the new institutions—the Russian
legislature and presidency, though not the Russian Communist Party—fatally undermined the Union. And, as
Yeltsin's success in fortifying alternative Russian republic

institutions became manifest, his constituency *at the top* expanded beyond a small group of naïve, inexperienced 'democrats' to officials of the USSR state, who saw a chance either to preserve or to increase their power.[30]

A similar, and equally decisive, evolution took place in Ukraine. In mid-1990, Leonid Kravchuk, who was about to become the Ukrainian parliament leader, announced his support for the Union Treaty, commenting that 'to live outside the Soviet Union, means to lose a great deal, if not everything'. By the autumn of 1990, however, after Ukrainian students had gone on a hunger strike for independence—an act that helped bring down the inept Ukrainian government—Kravchuk began insisting that any ties to Moscow would have to be in accordance with Ukraine's declaration of sovereignty. In November 1990 he concluded a bilateral agreement with Russia that recognized each republic's sovereignty. When, in the spring of 1991, the second draft of the Union Treaty came under discussion, Kravchuk, by then eyeing a run for a new Ukrainian presidency, rejected it outright. And the more he seemed capable of claiming the nationalist turf from the small but vocal nationalist groups, the more the upper strata of the survival-minded Ukrainian elite closed ranks behind him.[31]

That the Union's demise was 'national in form, opportunist in content' was equally evident in Kazakhstan. In June 1989 Nursultan Nazarbaev became Kazakh party chief, and in April 1990 he was elected chairman of the Kazakhstan Supreme Soviet. Later that year, Nazarbaev was nominated for the post of USSR Vice-President, but he demurred. Along with his supporters in the Kazakhstan elite, he manipulated nationalism to consolidate power in the republic, yet, even during his campaign for the new Kazakh presidency in late 1991, Nazarbaev resisted calls for complete independence. True, the irrepressible problems created by the disarray in the planned economy as well as the increasing dysfunction of Union ministries compelled even reluctant republican leaders to assume ever-greater responsibilities for economic crisis management, communications, customs, and many other duties. But 'up until the very last minute', one scholar has concluded, 'almost all of Central Asia's leaders maintained hope that the Union could be saved', at least in some guise.[32]

Thus, it was not nationalism *per se*, but the structure of the Soviet state—fifteen national republics—that proved fatal to the USSR, primarily because nothing was done to prevent that structure's use and misuse. 'Reform' involved intentional devolution of authority to the republics, but that process was radicalized by the decision not to intervene in 1989 in Eastern Europe and by Russia's assault against the Union. Even so, the dissolution of the Union was not inevitable. In India during the 1980s and 1990s the central authorities killed many thousands of separatists in the name of preserving the integrity of the state, at little or no cost to the country's democratic reputation.[33] The Indian government consistently issued unambiguous signals about what lines could not be crossed, and used force against secessionist movements that crossed them. The Soviet leadership under Gorbachev not only failed to draw clear lines, but also unintentionally spread nationalism itself. The *irresolute* spilling of blood, in Georgia in 1989 and Lithuania in early 1991, served as a formidable weapon in the hands of separatists, helping them recruit 'nationalists' among those who had been undecided, while placing Moscow on the defensive and demoralizing the KGB and army.

It was the central elite, rather than the independence movements of the periphery, that cashiered the Union. Had the putschists been effective, they would surely have rallied many of the middle and upper layers of the vast Soviet elite to the cause of preserving at least the core of the Union. But their blatantly botched crackdown instead widened the divisions in the elite that Yeltsin had opened up by his Russian presidential campaign, alongside the Union president, and by declaring the existence of a separate 'Russian republic military command' and a separate 'Russian republic KGB'. After the failed putsch, Yeltsin arrested some fifteen officials and compelled Gorbachev to remove others for suspected complicity. But many hundreds of thousands of USSR officers and officials made their way to safety in the Russian Federation. Thus, the larger truth about 1991 was that the 'triumph' of democracy involved a bid for power by Russian republic officials, joined at various points by patriots and opportunists from the all-Union elite—a process paralleled in Ukraine, Kazakhstan, and other national components of the Union.

Anyone who has been caught in a landslide knows the value of a large tree that suddenly comes into view and is solidly rooted. Some caught on right away, others later.

Counter-putsch

Every republic that had yet to declare independence did so either during or not long after the putsch—except Russia, which was manœuvring to become the legal heir to the Union, while also keeping alive the possibility of some inter-republican arrangements. Yeltsin advanced Russia's hostile takeover of Soviet institutions, yet he and several other republic heads continued to negotiate with Gorbachev. None of the 'agreements' reached at the sessions, however, was honoured outside the room. Then, in late September, Yeltsin, apparently ill, disappeared for seventeen days 'on vacation'. He returned in a decisive mood, appointing a 35-year-old economics professor, Yegor Gaidar, to lead the Russian government. To overcome the deadlock over the destroyed planned economy, amid warnings of a looming famine, Gaidar pressed for a Russian leap to the market independent of the indecisive Union Treaty negotiations or the conflicting policies of other republics. Among his first acts, he simply informed the USSR Planning Commission that it was under Russian jurisdiction and ordered that it plan steep reductions in arms production for 1992—and the functionaries obeyed. The Yeltsin entourage also annexed the Soviet finance ministry, mint, Academy of Sciences, and archives. Many observers labelled these actions a 'counter-putsch'.[34]

Yeltsin was not alone in undermining the Union. Kravchuk, while taking steps to claim Soviet military personnel and equipment on Ukrainian soil for a Ukrainian army, also announced a referendum on independence for 1 December. About 90 per cent voted in favour; there were large pro-independence majorities in the ethnically Russian provinces of Eastern Ukraine. Even in the third Slavic republic, Belarussia, the pro-Union yet survivalist leadership declared its independence after the putsch, while sponsoring a hasty name change to Belarus. The Belarus leader, Stanislav Shushkevich, lobbied Yeltsin to cut a deal with Gorbachev. But, whereas Yeltsin at least attended the Union Treaty negotiations, Kravchuk did not. On 5 December Yeltsin told journalists that a Union Treaty without Ukraine would be impossible. The Union seemed dead, but the republic leaders could not figure out how to get rid of the Soviet president. An opportunity to resolve the uncertainty arose with a previously scheduled bilateral Russia–Belarus meeting near Minsk for 7 December, which Kravchuk agreed to attend. The night before the three-way gathering, one of Yeltsin's top advisers sought out an acquaintance, the head of an American NGO in Moscow, to try to clarify the difference between a commonwealth, a federation, and a confederation.[35]

Aides to the three leaders worked most of the next day and night. At noon on 8 December, they suddenly sought to contact Nazarbaev, who turned out to be on a plane to

Moscow for a meeting with Gorbachev scheduled for 9 December. Without Nazarbaev, the three Slavic leaders announced that, 'since the USSR is ceasing to exist', they had established a Commonwealth of Independent States (CIS). The CIS had no common parliament, president, or citizenship, only a vague pledge to work on collective security. Shushkevich was assigned to call Gorbachev, but only after Yeltsin had called US President George Bush. Not long before the August 1991 putsch, Bush had delivered his 'chicken-Kiev' speech in the Ukrainian capital, where he had warned against 'suicidal nationalism', but, in an about face, Washington leaked that it would recognize Ukrainian independence sometime after the 1 December referendum. As always, Gorbachev had been counting on the leverage of an enormous Western aid package.[36] Instead, Bush became one of the last of the opportunists to abandon the Union for the republics.

On 10 December, after the announcement of the CIS, Gorbachev, still technically commander in chief, appealed to the military high command, but the next day the generals received Yeltsin and chose to back him as the real power and the only hope for salvaging a unified Armed Forces. On 21 December a meeting to expand the amorphous CIS to eleven members—all but Georgia and the three Baltic republics—took place in the Kazakh capital. The leaders of the Central Asian republics, Belarus and Russia, hoped, each for its own reasons, that the CIS would become a workable entity, but the Ukrainian leadership wanted merely to bury the Soviet state, which the assembled republic leaders formally dissolved. Two days later Gorbachev met Yeltsin and agreed to step down as USSR president. On 25 December the red hammer and sickle was lowered from the Kremlin, and replaced by the red, white, and blue flag of Russia. On 27 December, four days prior to the date Gorbachev was supposed to vacate his Kremlin office, the receptionist called him at home to report that Yeltsin and two associates were already squatting in the coveted space, where they had downed a celebratory bottle of whisky. It was 8.30 a.m.

Long fearing the 'conservatives', Gorbachev had mesmerized and browbeaten them at party forums and behind the scenes with what must have been intoxicating wizardry. In the attempt to re-energize the system, he had led them into territory they had never imagined; they hated him for it, but were petrified of being left without him. After he drew close to them in late 1990 only to semi-abandon them in April 1991, they finally acted, yet their scheme was based on his willingness to join in! Yeltsin was a different matter. He would have been eaten alive in Gorbachev's position. But he achieved what Gorbachev never dared: power rooted securely in the ballot box. If Yeltsin's memoirs cannot conceal the fact that Gorbachev grudgingly provided him with the possibility of office, and the cover for reckless taunting of the Soviet establishment, Gorbachev's cannot disguise his misplaced scorn: the world renowned lion-tamer of the establishment was upstaged by the guy who climbs out of the Volkswagen. In the end, the Russian president proved too spiteful and the Soviet president too vain for the two to embrace each other and save some form of the Union, yet their complementary roles helped defang a dangerous, well-armed police state.

Looking back at the putsch, some commentators cite Gorbachev's 'failure' to break out of the Crimean dacha and discrepancies in when communications were halted to suggest a wait-and-see complicity.[37] Chief Investigator Evgenii Lisov concluded that Gorbachev had offered no hints, obliquely or directly, to suggest that he was with the plotters, but they nonetheless calculated he would join them after a few days. We may never learn the full story. The more important point is that at various times Gorbachev might have tried to institute martial law and did not. Flabbergasted by the fact that his socialist renewal was leading to the system's liquidation, Gorbachev more or less went along. In sanctimonious, selective, and occasionally distorted reminiscences, he presents this acquiescence as an activist strategy—a disingenuous and, ultimately, superfluous exercise. Yugoslavia's bloody break-up, as well as the careers of Slobodan Milosevic, Franjo Tudjman, and their tinpot henchmen, will forever provoke additional shudders over how events might have turned out across northern Eurasia and the satellites of Eastern Europe.

5

Survival and cannibalism in the rust belt

[The Soviet economy's] past is written into the composition and location of its capital stock, the patterns of its roads and railroads, the size and type of its plants, the distribution of its manpower, the kinds of fuel it burns and ore it uses. Even a perfect leader and a perfect reform, whatever those might be, could not right in a generation what has taken two generations to form.

(Thane Gustafson, Russia specialist, 1989)

'I think', says Ivan to Volodya, 'that we have the richest country in the world'.
'Why?' asks Volodya.
'Because for nearly sixty years everyone has been stealing from the state and still there is something left to steal.'

(Hedrick Smith, *The Russians*, 1976)

At the end of George Orwell's 1945 'fairy tale', *Animal Farm*, something extraordinary occurs. Recall that having overthrown Mr Jones in the Great Rebellion, the animals of Manor Farm set about building a new world without exploitation when the pigs, who assumed a leading role, announce they are moving from the communal barn into Mr Jones's old manor house. The pigs even take to wearing clothes and walking on two legs. Such a turn of events, the pigs insist, is absolutely in keeping with the spirit of the Rebellion and in any case is vital, because all the surrounding farms are still run by people, and remain hostile. Sure enough, a neighbour, Mr Frederick, attacks with his men. Entering into an alliance with another human neighbour, Mr Pilkington, Animal Farm survives Frederick's onslaught.

To celebrate their improbable, draining victory, the pigs host a visit of their wartime human ally. Curious, the rest of Animal Farm's creatures, who live badly yet retain a sense of honour as inhabitants of the world's only farm owned and operated by the animals themselves, huddle against the outer windows of the manor. Looking in, they discover an uncanny resemblance between the pigs and people. They also overhear Mr Pilkington compliment the pig leader, Napoleon (Caesar in the French translation), for the low rations, long working hours, and absence of pampering of the lower animals on Animal Farm. Gratified, Napoleon squeals that the pigs have just decided to abolish the outmoded revolutionary name Animal Farm and revert to the original Manor Farm!

Orwell vividly captured the betrayal of the people by the elites as a key characteristic of the Soviet regime, but he got it only half right. Much of the Communist upper class, enjoying *de facto* ownership of state-owned property, mocked its slogans about the proletariat and social justice, yet, even four decades after Orwell's masterpiece, segments of the Soviet elite resisted abandoning the spirit and practice of the Animal Farm ideology. Once Gorbachev's reforms broke everything loose, however, even ideologue 'pigs' got swept up in the pursuit of property. The KGB and the army began wheeling and dealing commodities, from arms to computers, for institutional and private profit. The Central Committee, still railing against the market, also established private businesses. Individually, officials signed over to themselves deeds for state dachas, vehicles, anything under their watch, at bargain prices, if they paid at all. In the words of one penetrating analyst, those in power 'rushed to claim . . . assets before the bureaucratic doors shut for good'.[1] In fact, the doors to property appropriation and self-enrichment were only just opening. As the republics cast aside the Union carcass and a rapid turn to the market became official policy in Russia, the seizure of the state-owned wealth of the USSR evolved into frenzy.

Most ordinary people had anticipated the onset of American-style affluence, combined with European-style social welfare. After all, these were the rosy images of the outside world, transmitted by glasnost, which had helped destroy what was left of their allegiance to socialism. But instead, the people got an economic involution and mass impoverishment combined with a headlong expansion of precisely what had helped bring down the Soviet Union—the squalid appropriation of state functions and state property by Soviet-era elites. Some functionaries ripped out the phones, carpets, and wood panelling before fleeing. But most returned to their old desks, or reshuffled to new ones, and used their official duties—licensing power, affixing of state seals, authorizing or blocking investigations—to enrich themselves far more than they could or would have under Communism. Thus did the lead Zeppelin of post-Communist euphoria crash and burn, and the finger pointing begin.

Numerous analysts blamed the supposedly dogmatic monetarist reforms, which were derided as 'Thatcherism' and 'market Bolshevism'.[2] But these critics neglected to *demonstrate* that Russia underwent ruthless neo-liberal reforms. It did not. Nor could it have. The same goes for pie-in-the-sky alternatives. Critics of Russia's rhetorical neo-liberalism failed to specify *who* was supposed to have implemented their suggested state-led 'gradualist' policies—the millions of officials who had betrayed the Soviet state and enriched themselves in the bargain? No Russian leadership, rising to power by virtue of the spiralling collapse of central (Soviet) state institutions, could have prevented the ensuing total appropriation of bank accounts and property that the state owned on paper, but that were in the hands of unrestrained actors. Of course, members of the Yeltsin inner circle and his appointed government, unable to halt the mass expropriations, did not even try to do so. Far from it—top officials pumped out decrees and orders that brought them lucre. But so did their subordinates, and their subordinates' subordinates, while factory directors reclassified profitable operations inside 'their' factories and pocketed the proceeds, a legalization and enlargement of long-standing black-market practices.

The infinite variety of scams that came to the surface eloquently testified to entrepreneurial skills acquired from decades of having engaged in 'extra-plan' dealings for both plan fulfilment and personal gain. Now, there was no plan. And there was no Communist Party discipline to enforce even a meagre degree of control. There was, however, a ten-time-zone Russian rust belt, whose combination of economic deadweight and scavenging opportunities defined the decade of the 1990s. Nothing revealed the bankruptcy of the late Soviet Union more than the bankruptcy of post-Soviet Russia. The country's predicament was, therefore, not some supposed 'cultural' lack or peculiarity, or an excess of bad foreign advice, or a small band of thieving 'oligarchs'.[3] It was a problem of institutions, as the story of Russia's economic 'reforms' in this chapter demonstrates, and as the story of Russia's mishmash political order in the next chapter sums up. The Soviet collapse continued throughout the 1990s, and much of what appeared under the guise of reform involved a cannibalization of the Soviet era.

The illusions of reform . . .

Yegor Gaidar had an impeccable Soviet pedigree. Grandson of perhaps the Soviet Union's best-loved children's writer, son of a top *Pravda* correspondent, he grew up abroad in Tito's Yugoslavia. As a teenager in the late 1960s, Gaidar claims to have read a 1938 edition of Adam Smith, Paul Samuelson's basic economics textbook, and, more importantly, a Marxist indictment of property monopolization, *The New Class*, by the former second in command to Tito, Milovan Djilas. Gaidar also acquired first-hand experience of Yugoslavia's touted industrial management reforms. At university in Moscow in the 1970s, Gaidar claims he read the copies of John Maynard Keynes, John Galbraith, and Milton Friedman kept in the library's 'secret collection', as well as Marx. More practically, he closely studied Hungary's 'goulash Communism', with its small private sector. By his own telling, Gaidar remained 'an orthodox Marxist'. But he wondered—like Gorbachev, whom he had advised on perestroika's Yugoslav–Hungarian inspired 1987–8 economic reforms—how to escape the cul-de-sac whereby state socialism empowered a sclerotic bureaucracy while 'market socialism' proved difficult to realize in practice. As of November 1991, however, when Boris Yeltsin tapped the academic to head the Russian government, all that was moot. 'We were in a situation', Gaidar later admitted, 'where theory was powerless'.[4]

In 1991 the budget deficit would exceed 20 per cent of

estimated GDP, and 1992 threatened to be worse (it was). Soviet gold reserves and foreign currency accounts had disappeared, never to be found. Soviet foreign debt had ballooned to $56.5 billion, and creditors were demanding that the successor states assume full responsibility. Only Russia did so—the price extracted for the Soviet seat on the UN Security Council—assuming a formidable burden at a time when the rouble was undergoing steep devaluation.[5] Russian industry was in free fall, caught between plan and market and politically severed from suppliers and customers in Eastern Europe as well as the other Union republics. The officially measured economy declined 6 per cent in 1990 and an annualized 17 per cent through the first three-quarters of 1991. (In the worst year of the Great Depression in the US, 1929–30, the drop was 9 per cent.) Inflation at the end of 1991 was estimated at 250 per cent—per month. Enterprises refused payments in roubles, insisting instead on foodstuffs, vodka, or televisions, especially of foreign origin, which could be distributed to workers in lieu of money wages. Shops were emptier than at any time since the famine years immediately after the Second World War. Before Gaidar had lifted a finger, Russia was utterly broke and in chaos.

He and his team—a mix of arrogant Young Turk 'economists', mediocre political operatives from Yeltsin's hometown, and old-hand former Soviet ministers—hoped to impose monetary stabilization through fiscal discipline, while also crushing the remnants of the planning system and clearing a path for market behaviour. The Russian programme was advertised as 'shock therapy', on the example of 1990 Poland and 1970s Chile, by the International Monetary Fund, which was unhurriedly negotiating a large dollar loan to support Russia's 'transition', and by a handful of self-promoting foreign advisers. But the idea of de-statization and painful belt tightening as the path from socialism to the market derived not from foreign models but from Russia's dire circumstances and Soviet-era conceptions about the market being the opposite of the planned economy. Gaidar, in any case, violated shock therapy, conceding that some prices, such as those for bread and milk, would remain regulated, to protect the population. Others in government insisted that liberalization of energy and fuel prices be 'delayed', to 'protect' Russian industry and enable the country to survive the winter, and Gaidar acceded to the pressure.

On 2 January 1992 Russia ended most but far from all Soviet-era administered prices in what was dubbed 'a single leap across the abyss'. Overnight, private trade ceased to be the crime of 'speculation', and the country was soon transformed into a bustling bazaar of buyers and sellers on street corners. People who bought what turned out to be unusable goods had no recourse, but shop queues disappeared and the goods famine was overcome. Monetary stabilization, however, proved elusive. President Yeltsin toured the country with hundreds of millions of roubles in cash, which he magnanimously distributed to the folk like the tsars of old.[6] Even worse, the Soviet State Bank was replaced by fifteen republic Central Banks, but the currency—the rouble—was retained, under the mistaken view among some Russian officials and the IMF that a single 'rouble zone' would promote economic reintegration. Only Russia's Central Bank, having inherited all Soviet printing presses, could issue paper roubles, but crazily, all republic banks could issue credits in roubles. 'In effect,' wrote one journalist for *Rolling Stone*, 'Russia had fourteen ex-wives, each with a duplicate of the Kremlin Visa card'.[7]

Fiscal pressure also emanated from Soviet-era industry. Inter-enterprise debts soared to 800 billion roubles by March 1992, and by July reached 3.2 trillion roubles—a quarter of Russian GDP. It was as if firms were issuing money (credits) to each other, appropriating the powers of the central authorities. Gaidar, who had written his Ph.D. on the benefits expected from granting autonomy to firms, now watched as autonomous firms awarded themselves free money. Their unilateral debt expansion, moreover, became a powerful lobbying tool for extracting the government subsidies that he had denied them. Trapped, Gaidar caved in to new outlays, and between July and September credits to industry blew giant holes in his tight money policy. Inflation, which, despite the CIS banking fiasco and Yeltsin's largesse, had been reduced to around 7–9 per cent per month in July 1992, jumped by the autumn to 25 per cent a month. So much for implementing dogmatic monetarism!

At the same time that Gaidar struggled to impose fiscal discipline, the entire Soviet epoch, no longer shielded by autarky, was being brutally re-evaluated by the world market. Life savings in roubles that had had a certain value in the Soviet era were, in the new circumstances, wiped out. Rouble pensions for millions of people who had worked all their lives became almost worthless. The salaries of highly educated professionals—physicians, scholars—became microscopic. Amid this impoverishment, opponents of 'reform' proved far better at framing public debate than proponents, who exhibited a we-know-best distain for public explanation and naïvety about the power of cynical exploitation of public relations. In a great irony, it was not the Soviet past but 'reform' that was compelled to stand trial. And, even before the IMF fiscal stabilization loans came through, belatedly, in July—despite Russia's failure to meet the conditions set down—critics bitter about the fall of the Union accused Washington of a second 'global plot', this one to strangle Russian industry. Hounded in the press and parliament, Gaidar barely survived an attempt to sack him in April 1992, but in December he was forced out.

Some analysts were quick to defend shock therapy, arguing that it had not been implemented strictly. That was true. But of what utility was an economic programme said to work only in pure form when even its advocates warn of real-world obstacles during implementation? The theorists, anticipating strikes, called for the introduction of a social safety net; this was not done, yet there were few strikes. Instead, the social pressures came from managerial elites. Bosses of the tens of thousands of large enterprises built in the Soviet period, explains one Gaidar associate, 'possessing material, labour, and financial resources, and being better organized than anyone else', emerged as a dominant political force in policymaking.[8] Gaidar had galvanized them, first by setting managers free from the remaining controls of the planning bureaucracy, then by seeking to cut them off from state credits. When they fought back, the would-be shock therapist sought to co-opt them with inflationary credits, but they turned against him anyway. After leaving government, Gaidar admitted having acquired in office 'an infinitely better idea of how real power works'.[9]

The era of 'radical reform' was pronounced over. Russia's new head of government, the Soviet-era gas minister Viktor Chernomyrdin, stoked Western doomsday prophecies by bemoaning the steep decline of industry. But Chernomyrdin ended up, despite vacillations and occasional reversals, implementing a more vigorous anti-inflationary course than Gaidar had. This apparent mystery is readily explained. First, in July 1993, Russia finally managed to achieve what Gaidar had demanded: it cut the other former Soviet republics off from issuing rouble credits, and replaced the Soviet rouble with a new Russian rouble. Secondly, Chernomyrdin hit a brick wall. Myriad opponents of shock therapy who claimed that Gaidar should have tried a gradual reform approach, directing credits to priority industries, overlooked the fact that his successor attempted to do just that—and failed. Chernmyrdin discovered that neither the government nor the Central Bank had sufficient authority to enforce investment priorities at the level of enterprises. He also came to understand that free-flowing state credits—'the opiate of industry'—caused harmful inflation. And so, with the assistance of the finance minister, the personification of the industrial lobbies embraced a policy of tighter credits and fiscal stabilization.[10]

Russia achieved a gradual monetary stabilization. Inflation declined from 2,250 per cent in 1992, to 840 per cent in 1993, to 224 per cent in 1994, and by September 1996 to an annualized rate near zero, thereafter for the most part remaining low. Just as Gaidar had come to understand basic politics, Chernomyrdin had come to understand basic economics. One of his successors as prime minister, Yevgeny Primakov (1998–9), using an even more 'patriotic' rhetoric about reviving industry, sponsored an even tighter budget and credit policy. There was little else that the central government could effectively do.[11] For Russia, which struggled just to gain full control over its money supply, carrying out comprehensive economic 'reform' was an illusion. And therefore, Western advice, whether misguided or sensible, was largely inconsequential. Russia's was not, and could not have been, an engineered transition to the market. It was a chaotic, insider, mass plundering of the Soviet era, with substantial roots prior to 1991, and ramifications stretching far into the future.

. . . and the realities of marketeering

In the 1970s, the USSR, through oil exports and grain imports, became more involved in the world economy, but it still accounted for a minuscule 1.5 per cent of world trade into the 1980s. Under the planned economy, there were gaping differentials between domestic fixed prices and world market prices—oil, for example, was priced domestically at less than 1 per cent of the world price—but, since foreign trade in the Soviet Union was a state monopoly, the windfall revenues went to the state budget. Already in 1986, however, a number of ministries besides the Ministry of Foreign Economic Relations had successfully lobbied for permission to engage in foreign trade, and soon this privilege was extended to select enterprises and even individuals, usually with the proviso that they would use export revenues to import goods in short supply.[12] Exporters failed to live up to their contracts to overcome consumer shortages. Instead, they accumulated fortunes that were hidden abroad by using mechanisms that the KGB had developed to pay for industrial espionage: channelling funds through shell companies as well as banks in offshore locations. In other words, well before 1991, a pattern had been set.

Russia was even more desperate to overcome still worse shortages, including those of sugar and soap, and it further 'liberalized' foreign trade. But domestic energy prices remained under government fiat. In the summer of 1993 Russian prices for natural gas were still only 10 per cent of the world price (rising to 20 per cent by December 1993), while as late as 1994 domestic oil prices were still less than half world price. This meant, ironically, that, pursuing trade 'liberalization', the Russian government became even more involved in the intrigue of granting exclusive export licences. Predictably, the country rarely saw the promised medicines or children's clothes. 'There were', Gaidar wrote, 'always colossal numbers of opportunists buzzing around the government, proposing what seemed, at first glance, attractive projects'. He added, protectively, that his close friend, Russia's minister of foreign economic relations, who signed the export licences, 'had never held a government post, and the only thing he'd ever supervised was his own desk'.[13] Cluelessness was not the main problem (and anyway, Gaidar's team was soon out). The main problem was that Russian officials used their positions of public power to pursue their private interests.[14]

For official documents, bureaucrats 'practically have a price list hanging on the office wall', in the words of a Soviet-era convict who was handed assets to form one of Russia's biggest 'banks'.[15] Often state officials themselves set up the private companies. And just try to fight it! Firms denied export licences simply exported restricted, price-controlled goods by invoicing them as children's toys or teapots and 'coming to terms' with customs inspectors. Goods that Gaidar had crossed off the price-control list in draft documents reappeared in final versions to be signed by the president. In 1994 Chernomyrdin 'limited' price-controlled exports to petroleum products, natural gas, non-ferrous metals, timber, and fish—commodities that accounted for 70 per cent of exports. Amid this mar-keteering, vastly greater sums of capital fled Russia than the IMF ever loaned to it. Most large-scale exporters vio-lated Russia's currency repatriation laws, but more nimble ones took advantage of the tax treaty that the Soviet Union had signed with Cyprus—again as a means for the KGB to channel clandestine funds—which no one had repealed.[16]

Among the new loopholes created was an 'offshore' zone inside Russia, in the North Caucasus republic of Ingushetia, ostensibly to encourage investment. Com-panies registered in Ingushetia had to pay 'fees' to the Ingush authorities and their Moscow partners, but then legally thumbed their noses at Russia's tax authorities. Perhaps the biggest con involved the National Sports Foundation (NSF), set up by President Yeltsin's tennis coach for 'destitute Olympic athletes' and allowed to import sports equipment, then alcohol and cigarettes, duty free. The NSF accounted for 95 per cent of imported tobacco and spirits, and raked in more than $1.8 billion in a few years. Athletes saw none of these profits. As other 'charities' scrambled to ape the NSF example, the defin-ition of charity was stretched when the gas monopoly, formerly run by Prime Minister Chernomyrdin, was granted tax exemptions worth $4 billion in 1993 alone. Staggering fortunes were amassed, beginning at the top and extending down intricate 'loot chains' to the lowliest beneficiaries.

The lawlessness throughout officialdom was paralleled by an increase in lawlessness on the streets. In 1994 alone, more than 600 businessmen, journalists, and politicians were murdered in bombings and grenade attacks over 'market share'. In effect, a mega-merger had taken place among the vast surpluses of Soviet-era ex-convicts, sportsmen, and KGB operatives, who formed extortion rackets or private security forces—which were often the same thing.[17] But talk of 'the mafia' could be confused. Not the plentiful private criminal groups, but those working for the state engaged in the greatest extortion. For people in business, it was well nigh impossible to be honest even if they wanted to be. Much foreign trade involved not government-licensed grand larceny or gangland racketeering, but un-licensed modest shuttle traders, who travelled abroad by passenger train, bus, private car, even chartered aeroplane, returning with suitcases of otherwise unavailable goods, which they resold to eager consumers. The small-fry entrepreneurs struggled to avoid taxes, which were confiscatory, and to lessen customs duties by paying bribes. The more successful their business became, however, the greater the shakedowns by state officials.

Strictly speaking, this was not corruption, which presupposes the prevalence of rule-regulated behaviour, so that violators are identified and prosecuted. Rather, this was 'pre-corrupt', a condition whereby everyone to varying degrees was a violator, but only the weak were targeted. Imagine Wall Street—corrupt as it is already—if regulation were non-existent. Or American business if regulations functioned merely as a pretext for the petty to extract 'fines' and the powerful to crush competitors and those without connections. Try starting a business, and competing against other businesses, without publicly maintained roads, a government-overseen banking and credit system, a powerful state agency to curb monopolies, or a well-policed police force, to say nothing of safety for workers and protection for consumers against swindles and diseases. Capitalism without government regulation or with random and manipulated government was not pretty. But, like insider enrichment and conflation of the public and the private, it had a long, illustrious history, and it still predominated across the world. Russia, paradoxically, needed both far, far deeper economic liberalization, and much better government regulation.

The ambiguities of property . . .

In addition to Gaidar's abortive monetary stabilization and partial price liberalization, the other lever for achieving the 'transition' from Soviet socialism was privatization. Crafted by a different Young Turk political economist, Anatoly Chubais, and funded largely by relatively minor Western grants, Russia's privatization programme wended through the full bureaucratic maze for suggestions and approvals, and then after considerable debate was passed in general form into law by the Supreme Soviet in mid-1992. Of course, *de facto* appropriation of state property and asset stripping by factory directors were already very far advanced. Unable to reverse this mass opportunism of self-privatization, Chubais schemed to institutionalize and rationalize it. He also aimed to make regional and municipal governments self-interested beneficiaries by 'delegating' to them something he could not have over-seen: privatization of hundreds of thousands of small-scale businesses. Chubais and his handful of associates concen-trated on a 'mass' privatization of large firms—in a land with more than 15,000 such state enterprises, and without accumulations of private investor capital.

Between October 1992 and February 1993, a time of extreme catastrophic stagflation, every man, woman, and child in Russia, nearly 150 million people, received a voucher with a nominal value of 10,000 roubles—first worth $25, soon worth around $2—to be used in property auctions. In anticipation of public sale, all large state firms were compelled to become incorporated, but as open joint-stock companies, to pre-empt the formation by insiders of collective-farm-style closed partnerships resist-ant to economic modernization. Vouchers were made tradeable, permitting the acquisition of significant share blocks by 'outsiders', in the hope that they would pressure firms to become viable in market conditions. Tirelessly working through the myriad technicalities of history's largest ever property re-registration and sale, the Chubais group was guided by political goals: to beat back anti-private property forces in the parliament and media; to win over existing stakeholders (the sticky-fingered managers, many of whom opposed legal privatization for fear they would lose *de facto* ownership); and to create millions of new stakeholders in capitalism.

Shrewdly adapted to circumstances, privatization was also, by design, a mad rush. In the chaos that constituted the still forming Russian state, Chubais, like Gaidar, believed that he had a unique chance to knock out Soviet-era economic structures, and that such an opportunity was destined not to last.[18] The first auction held by the State Property Committee—of the Bolshevik Biscuit Company —took place in December 1992, only days before Gaidar's government was forced to resign. Chubais survived into the new Chernomyrdin government, but most of the implementation of mass privatization was ahead. In 1993, when one province threatened to prohibit privatization on its territory, threatening a domino effect, Chubais flew there, perorated on regional television and at work collectives, and forced the authorities to back down. That same year the Property Committee's offices in Moscow were stormed in a mêlée, but $55 million worth of spent vouchers, bundled together with unused condoms, went untouched. The intruders either did not notice the vouchers, or did not understand their value.[19]

Foreign consultants on the privatization staff sought a very high profile, rendering the process vulnerable to charges of being a 'Western plot', but foreign investors were excluded from the bidding, in a supposed bow to nationalists who decried the sale of Russia's 'patrimony'. That exclusion robbed Russia of a critical lever for assessing, and perhaps raising the worth of, its patrimony. The AvtoVAZ carmaker, for example, was purchased at voucher auction for $45 million, whereas in 1991 Fiat had offered $2 billion—and been turned away. Between 1992 and 1996, according to an investigation of hundreds of companies, on average factory management *admitted* paying about forty times less than their companies were supposedly worth. The investigators noted that the voucher value of *all* Russian industry—including some of the world's richest deposits of natural resources—came to about $12 billion, less than the value at the time of Anheuser-Busch. Russian state property was given away for small beer, to make privatization an 'irreversible' political reality.[20]

Another key aim, precluding a collective-farm-like ownership structure geared to blocking outsiders, was mostly subverted. Offered three models by which to proceed, almost three-quarters of large firms chose the option whereby management and workers purchased a 51 per cent controlling block of their company's voting equity—a variant introduced by the parliament, and reluctantly accepted by Chubais to get the legislation through. True, the state—meaning federal, provincial, and/or municipal governments—kept substantial equity stakes in the economy, and in theory these shares could later be sold to 'strategic investors', who might demand painful restructuring even if work collectives and managers resisted. This was, perhaps unavoidably, an ambiguous outcome: the state was generally not a good owner (hence the drive to privatize in the first place), while the main method of private incorporation (majority employee ownership) could hinder market-oriented restructuring that presupposed mass lay-offs. Nonetheless, within just a few years some 15,000 large and mid-sized enterprises had been legally registered as 'privately owned'. In its sweeping scale and haste, the privatization was quintessentially Russian. But Russia had never had so much private property in its thousand-year existence.

A second stage of privatization (1995–8), involving enterprises in 'strategic' industries previously excluded, followed a very different approach. The central government, having difficulty collecting taxes and properly managing its finances, was running budget deficits, which newly established private banks offered to cover with 'loans' if, as collateral, the government would put up the shares it retained in oil, nickel manufacturing, and other coveted sectors. Only twenty-nine concerns were involved, but they were lucrative ones. Should the government fail to repay the loans—a sure bet—the shares would be sold at auction. Incredibly, Chubais allowed the private lenders themselves to run the auctions. Preserving the appearance of competition, the insider banks negotiated a division of spoils at fire-sale prices. Worse, they paid with capital acquired from their dubious commercial 'management' of government funds, such as federal tax receipts and federal customs duties, which should have been in government accounts. Thus, commercial interests were in effect 'loaning' the government its own money, and thereby acquiring strategic industries for free. 'Loans for shares', a poorly disguised, cynical ploy to create a top business elite loyal to the Yeltsin regime (facing re-election), discredited privatization even among many of its defenders.[21]

An even deeper problem than the perceived illegitimacy of privatization was its frequent irrelevance. By gaining managerial control over a majority state-owned company, well-connected types could simply 'privatize' cash flow— that is, outsource the handling of cash receipts for exorbitant fees to private companies they themselves owned. Another favourite trick was for managers to sell a firm's products below wholesale to themselves, in the guise of a middleman firm, and retail the goods at substantial profit. Managers at majority private-owned businesses did the same. Through such flimflam, thousands of Soviet-era firms were looted *independently* of their ownership status or the privatization process. Privatization did little to enable rank-and-file shareholders to defend their paper property rights. But larger institutional investors were winning some property rights battles, and the increasing public outcries over the need to guarantee property rights testified not only to the distance Russia still had to go, but also to how far it had come.

. . . *and the barter of the bankrupt*

Privatization was an end in itself but also a means to an end: economic renewal. Even the foreign consultants who trumpeted privatization as a 'rare success story of Russian economic reform' acknowledged that success would 'ultimately' be determined by 'the speed and scope of restructuring' of industry, which they admitted had barely 'begun'.[22] A later survey of Russian industry uncovered little evidence of restructuring, as well as negligible outsider influence over firms and substantial passive state ownership throughout the economy.[23] In 'loans for shares', privatized enterprises did get outside management, but they received virtually no new investment and were not significantly restructured (instead, their revenues were siphoned to fund other activities of the new owners). At the start of the 1990s, two-thirds of the factory equipment in Russia was judged obsolete, and one scholar, commenting in 1998, argued that the rate of capital stock obsolescence had since 'speeded up dramatically'.[24] The upshot should have been unprecedented plant closure, even worse than in the Western rust belt back in the 1970s.

Russian GDP, in a mere half decade, did shrink an eye-popping 50 per cent, according to official measurements. But Soviet economic output had been wildly over-reported to 'meet' plan targets. In post-Soviet Russia, it was under-reported to avoid taxes. No one knew the scope of post-1991 unregistered economic activity, which may have been equal to half the size, or more, of the measured economy. Electricity consumption did not decrease nearly as much as GDP. Unemployment was high (officially 12 per cent, probably closer to 20), but not commensurate with GDP decline. And employment patterns bespoke a surprise. Unlike in the West, where small and medium business accounted for two-thirds of employment, in mid-1990s Russia legally registered smaller enterprises employed no more than a tenth of the workforce.[25] Instead, large firms (those with more than 500 workers), which had accounted for about 83 per cent of production and employment in 1991, accounted for 78 per cent of official production and 63 per cent of official employment in 1996.[26] In other words, Russia's story was not just GDP decline. It was also the depressingly paltry number (even taking into account the underground economy) of new small businesses—whose proliferation in Poland provided the key to growth—as well as a continued socio-economic dependence on obsolete industrial giants.

While bureaucratic and credit barriers to opening and operating small businesses, the country's potential salvation, were inordinately high, thousands of Soviet-era factories, whose output was often worth *less* than the inputs they used, were somehow surviving. Tricking death, factories were shipping finished goods to their suppliers and customers even when not paid for, and their loss-making suppliers and customers cheerfully reciprocated. Such direct firm-to-firm dealings, sometimes in complex three- and four-way barter combinations, had helped Soviet enterprises illegally meet their plan targets. Now, mutual payment arrears, along with barter, held menacing market valuations at bay, and even allowed unprofitable enterprises to *expand*.[27] Worse, the circle of exchanging debts and in-kind payments entrapped potentially profitable

9a. The Soviet High Command, Red Square, 7 November 1989, just before the Berlin Wall was breached, and Eastern Europe was not prevented from breaking away. Only the commander of ground forces (second from left) would play an active role in the failed August 1991 putsch to 'save' the Union.

9b. Gorbachev with Chancellor Helmut Kohl, Stavropol, July 1990, when the Soviet leader voluntarily acceded to the unification of Germany with inclusion in NATO.

10. Boris Yeltsin, fist raised (centre). Having ridden to power atop a mass popular sentiment, Yeltsin retreated into a secluded, depressed, ineffectual rule, surrounded by courtiers, including bodyguard Alexander Korzhakov (behind and to the left of Yeltsin, looking down on the media).

11a. The Ukrainian flag was unfurled in the republic's Supreme Rada (parliament) on the day the deputies voted to declare independence, 24 August 1991. The majority of the Ukrainian elite came very late to the cause of independence. A statue of Lenin overlooks the proceedings.

11b. Armenian casualties of an Azerbaijani pogrom, which served as the rationale for Soviet military action in Baku, Azerbaijan, January 1990. The intervention took place after the pogroms had ended, and was designed to chasten nationalists and restore a pro-Moscow regime. By 1990–1, resolute use of force remained the only way of holding the Union together in order to try to transform it.

12a. Elite KGB troops, facing demonstrators and readying their truncheons, which they mordantly called 'democratizers'.

12b. The August 1991 coup plotters were a gang of eight, but not everyone showed up for their own press conference led by the unsteady Gennady Yanaev (right); missing were (left inset) the hardline prime minister Valentin Pavlov, who drank himself into the hospital, and (right inset) Defense Minister Yazov along with KGB chief Kryuchkov.

13a. Anatoly Chubais, chief of the State Property Committee responsible for privatization. To accompany his gesture (palms spread)—normally associated with the tall tales of fishermen who embellish the size of their catch—one of Chubais' many enemies appended a caption, 'everyone will receive a voucher this big'.

13b. Having saved her girlhood locks, a woman sells them at a specialty shop in St Petersburg. Her monthly pension was reduced to $16 by hyperinflation; her hair, worth slightly more, would be exported to the West for wig-making.

14a. Wide diameter pipes for siphoning off Russia's wealth (they went to build a new gas pipeline, early 1980s). Under Brezhnev, Gosplan invested prodigiously in the gas industry, and after 1991 the gas monopoly, a state within the state, provided one-fifth of the Russian government's budget revenues, despite highly dubious tax breaks and phenomenal embezzlement by management, linked to the prime minister.

14b. Deadly toxins from nickel mining and smelting plants waft over the Arctic city of Norilsk, 1990s. The factories in Norilsk constitute the world's single largest point source of sulfur dioxide emissions. They were built by Gulag (prison) labour and, after the Soviet dissolution, brought windfall export profits for management and then for new owners, a Moscow financial syndicate that concocted the infamous 'loans for shares' scam.

15a. T-72 tanks lined up for retreat. By fall 1994, from East Germany alone, the Russians withdrew more than 4,000 tanks, 1,300 planes and helicopters, 3,600 artillery pieces, 8,200 armored vehicles, and nearly 700,000 tons of ammunition (including nuclear-tipped shells), plus half a million soldiers and civilians (along the same corridor used by Napoleon during his infamous retreat in the opposite direction). Russia's was the biggest pullout ever by an army not defeated in war.

15b. Main entrance, the Central Committee's city within a city, 1991; a small crowd, concerned that evidence of party complicity in the August putsch was being destroyed, helped force the closure of the complex. Not long thereafter, the expansive CC site was reopened and again jammed with functionaries, having been rechristened the Presidential Administration.

16. Summit meeting of the Commonwealth of Independent States (CIS), which is neither a country nor a military alliance, nor a free trade zone, but a question mark.

firms, too. Keeping afloat the incurable had in a sense bankrupted everyone. Yet consider that almost *one half* of Russian towns had only one major industrial firm, and three-quarters no more than four. Such monopoly employers, moreover, also owned and often maintained urban mass transit systems, housing stock, hospitals, and winter heating systems.

Market logic was further stymied by bankruptcy proceedings being used for cut-rate hostile takeovers of profitable assets. When not colluding in such scams, regional governments bestowed various non-monetary subsidies on inefficient producers, claiming a need to maintain jobs and services. The federal authorities, too, were subsidizers, tolerating the tax arrears of energy supply companies so long as they maintained electricity to non-paying customers, such as military installations or giant employers.[28] Workers, even when paid only in kind or not at all, hung on, eating in factory canteens and scavenging factory tools and materials for their own private economic activities, as in Soviet times. If they were let go, workers kept their factory-built Soviet-era apartments, for which they paid only nominal fees for rent and utilities—any attempt to remove state budget subsidies for electricity, heat, and water just led to non-payments. In short, the Soviet legacy worked as a hindrance to full marketization, and as a safeguard against utter catastrophe.[29]

Soviet-era industry still dominated Russian employment, but major shifts occurred. For one thing, two-thirds of GDP was now in private hands. For another, the military's share plunged from around 20 per cent (in the mid-1980s) to under 5 per cent in 1998, while the energy sector's share climbed from 11 per cent in 1991 to 32 per cent by 1998. Russia became an export-dominated economy, but mostly of raw materials. Domestic oil production had dropped by half, yet consumption fell, too, enabling Russia to take advantage of high world oil prices during much of the decade. Even more crucial for the economy was the gas industry, which had been a top investment priority under Brezhnev. Chernomyrdin strengthened the gas sector's monopoly structure, while partially privatizing it with insiders. As a result, Russia's gas behemoth, despite utterly dubious tax breaks as well as breathtaking managerial embezzlement, supplied a fifth of federal budget revenues throughout the 1990s.[30] In a sense, the country was still living off its oil and gas—in a continuum since the 1970s. But, instead of underwriting a global military superpower, oil and gas financed far more modest levels of government spending and more immodest lifestyles of the reshuffled elites.

Oil and gas money also continued to encourage the delay of painful economic restructuring. Retooling obsolete plants costs considerably more than building new ones. In the former East Germany, factories—unable to ignore or outfox the market like their Russian counterparts—were not rebuilt; they were not even torn down but abandoned as new ones were built nearby, thanks to colossal capital transfers from a rich, condescending Western 'uncle'. Over the course of the 1990s in Russia, total direct foreign investment amounted to just several billion dollars per year, less than in tiny Hungary (which if somehow picked up and dropped from above into Russia could not be found again). No less important, Russia's banking system functioned not to make household savings available for productive investment but, periodically, to wipe savings out, and, with a big invisible hand from Western banks, to facilitate extensive money laundering and capital flight. Perhaps $150 billion of domestic capital fled Russia during the 1990s, an amount close to four times the IMF loans extended as 'aid'. Another $40 billion in domestic 'mattress savings' were also unavailable for investment.[31] The investment dearth was among the reasons that, even as Russia's continent of smokestacks connived to maintain its wasteful, toxic output, it continued to be cannibalized for short-term gain. Perhaps the only way to have 'restructured' Russia's rust belt was to have bombed it from the air.

Many analysts blamed the West, particularly the US, for not coming up with a Marshall Plan for Russia, but they were misguided on several counts.[32] In the late 1940s, Marshall money went to European bureaucrats who were strictly accountable and guided by rules to spend funds on imports not of consumer goods but of capital goods—a form of basic industrial policy excluded in the 1990s by the politically insurmountable American mythology of stateless markets. Also, the Marshall Plan sustained a West European recovery already underway. Russia was in a deep depression—an altogether different prospect. In any case, to offer the Russians—which Russians?—anything close to the investment necessary, the US government, even if it had miraculously overcome ideological objections, would have had to explain to American taxpayers how implementation was going to work, since Russia's own government failed miserably in efforts to direct investment, especially when compared to its successes in aiding capital flight. And what of accountability, in a country whose own Central Bank speculated against the rouble, hid money in offshore accounts, and spent hard-currency reserves on its own salaries, perquisites, and bureaucratic aggrandizement? The 'aid' (almost exclusively in the form of loans) that was extended to Russia predictably disappeared, leaving behind a mountain of public debt, just as had happened in Eastern Europe in the 1970s and 1980s, though Western governments later forgave much of Eastern Europe's debt.

In any event, all post-Communist countries, whether subjected to state-led gradualism or elements of shock therapy, saw GDP fall off a cliff. Ukraine held off price liberalization and its privatization was less far-reaching than Russia's, but its inflation and asset stripping were arguably worse, despite its free ride from not paying Russia for gas supplies. Certainly Russian policymakers can be blamed for not seeking to end the rouble zone immediately, for not removing controls on energy prices, and for trying to build political support with free state credits to industry. Certainly faking auctions to hand insiders strategic industries, just like facilitating foreign trade scams and using the gas industry as a private reserve, was unpardonable. But the underlying cause of Russia's difficulties was not policy. Rather, the fundamental factor was the Soviet bequeathal, one side of which was a socio-economic landscape dominated by white elephants that consumed labour, energy, and raw materials with little regard for costs or output quality.[33] The other side, remarkably, was even more ruinous: unfettered state officials whose larceny helped cashier the Soviet system, and whose bloated ranks swelled with many grasping newcomers.

Democracy without liberalism?

Just as you cannot have capitalism where everything is planned, so you cannot have capitalism where everything is for sale, not at least if the saleable items include employees at the public registry of titles and deeds. Markets presuppose a competent and honest bureaucracy ... [And] the idea that autonomous individuals can enjoy their private liberties if they are simply left unpestered by the public power dissolves before the disturbing realities of the new Russia.

> (Stephen Holmes, American political
> philosopher, 1997)

All my telephones were tapped. And I'm sure, not just the telephones.

> (Vyacheslav Kostikov, President Boris Yeltsin's
> loyal press secretary, 1997)

Well before Gorbachev came to power, it was evident that among Communism's greatest failures was its inability to control Communists. But who would have guessed that, after the elimination of the party from the state administration and well-intentioned democratic reforms, officialdom would become far more shameless under Yeltsin than it had been even under Brezhnev? Russia popularly elected and revamped its legislature, and popularly elected its president, even before the dissolution of the Union. But the country did not manage to cut back the number, or transform the behaviour, of the hordes of executive branch officials it inherited. Nor did it manage completely to overhaul the Soviet-era legal machinery, the Procuracy and the KGB, and sufficiently bolster the very weak Soviet-era judiciary. Democracy came to Russia atop the debris of the Soviet Union's expressly anti-liberal state, the institutional twin of the industrial planned economy.

Historically, liberalism—a legal order geared to the defence of private property and the civic rights of those recognized as citizens—combined the proclamation of universal principles with slavery or colonialism, and only very belatedly, after considerable struggle, extended legal protections, the right to form associations, and the franchise to all male inhabitants, and finally to women. But despite its glaring exclusions and deep flaws, liberalism, as Alexis de Tocqueville might have noted, is more fundamental to successful state building than democracy. Democratically elected office-holders, in multiparty systems, often behave like dictators unless they are constrained by a liberal order, meaning the rule of law. A liberal order involves a powerful parliament controlling the purse and issuing a steady stream of well-written laws, an authoritative judiciary to interpret and rule on the parliament's laws, and generally consistent implementation of laws and rules by a highly professional civil service, all of which allows for the influence of civic organizations to be felt. To put the matter another way, liberalism entails not freedom from government but constant, rigorous officiating of the private sphere and of the very public authority responsible for regulation. In short, liberalism —as is evident from its absence—means not just representative government but effective government, a geopolitical imperative for prosperity in the hierarchical world economy.

The Soviet system had served as a powerful shield against the dictates of the world economy. But that isolation could not have been maintained forever, and when it ended, its consequences proved especially disastrous. Furthermore, because the Soviet dictatorship had been distinguished by complete state ownership of property, the USSR, unlike even authoritarian inflections of historical liberalism, had had no corpus of laws for, or experience in, adjudicating legal private interactions among self-directed actors. True, the Soviet state had a huge body of laws, a court system, and legal experts, some of whom offered recourse to individuals wronged by state authorities. But innumerable executive decrees, many of them secret, asserted precedence over laws, and the executive power, if it so desired, could trump any court or legal decision, just as the executive commanded the legislature. The Soviet Union was governed by men, not laws. That was the very reason the Soviet executive power had an extremely difficult time governing *itself*.

Privatization in Russia was supposed to create a dynamic society and reduce the inordinate number and power of state officials. But it was precisely the members of Russia's arbitrary, unencumbered executive branch, at all levels, who assumed responsibility for history's most extensive privatization (which as of 2001 still had a considerable way to go), and over other key economic nodal points. Far from being snapped, the nexus between holding executive office and exercising control over property and resources was in some ways fortified. This circumstance enabled the executive power to eclipse legislatures, despite the latter's formal budgetary responsibilities, and it reduced Russian politics to a scrum to acquire and benefit from executive office, irrespective of ideological tilting. As individuals elected or appointed to positions of state authority pursued private gain to a greater degree, the commitment to the public good that had existed in the Soviet Union—for health care, education, children's summer camps—eroded much more deeply, demoralizing rather than empowering society.

This intensified privatization of public office and neglect of the public interest, both cause and effect of the Soviet collapse, were accompanied by a transience of formal organizations. From the late 1980s, a new political 'movement' was announced almost every week. By the end of the 1990s, Russia had nearly 100 registered 'political parties', but only one that was a real organization and countrywide—the relic Communists. Russia also had nearly a quarter of a million legally registered NGOs (until a forced 're-registration' reduced the number to around 100,000, still a hefty total). Yet, despite all the babble, dating back to the Gorbachev reforms, about the growth of 'civil society', none of Russia's NGOs came remotely close to matching the robustness and influence of the state-sponsored associations of the Communist period. Without empowering roots in society, state power was weak and it was unconstrained—except for the executive branch's own convoluted structures and officialdom's self-serving behaviour, both of which proved inimical not just to the tasks of facilitating a liberal, market society, but also to the aspirations of any would-be authoritarian ruler, whether Boris Yeltsin or his elected successor, Vladimir Putin.

Most Russia watchers were transfixed by Yeltsin's personal failings (he did finally apologize upon resigning slightly ahead of term), the chicanery of the 'oligarchs' (a misnomer for publicity-craving goniffs), hideous as well as pseudo nationalists (who also attracted broad media attention despite their lack of effective organizations), the supposed recalcitrance of the supposedly Communist-dominated legislature (which assiduously protected its perquisites by voting for initiatives of the Kremlin), and the ascent to power of former KGB agent Putin (a pragmatist uncertainly pursuing order amid chaos). Remarkably, analysts paid almost no attention to what really counted—the multiple institutions and mundane workings of the executive branch—even as these analysts looked to the executive branch to solve Russia's problems. Here was the fundamental quandary of successful 'reform', meaning something approaching a liberal order: how was the incoherent Russian state going to solve the country's problems when the state *was* the main problem?

Lame presidentialism

Think back to the spring and summer of 1989, a time when the first legislature worthy of that name came into being in the Soviet Union. It was an awkward two-tiered structure comprising a Congress of Peoples' Deputies—a kind of permanent Constitutional Convention—and a smaller 'working parliament', the Supreme Soviet, selected from the Congress. Importantly, the nomination made by the Congress's chairman (Gorbachev) for the post of prime minister was subject to a confirmation vote, after which he submitted nominees for other government posts to the deputies. Even the heads of the defence ministry and KGB, Yazov and Kryuchkov, had to appear and answer questions as part of the confirmation process. The two future putschists were confirmed, but some nominated ministers were rejected, and confirmed ministers could be called back any time to submit reports and answer questions. Lawmakers also formed committees that investigated the use of force on Soviet territory by the executive branch. Gorbachev's call for a law-based state—*pravovoe gosudarstvo*, akin to the continental notion of a *Rechtsstaat*—began to resonate.

But, having sidelined the Communist Party and transformed the parliament, Gorbachev found himself with only indirect levers over the Soviet legislature and the government. In March 1990, when he created a Soviet presidency, supposedly adapting the French hybrid presidential–parliamentary system, the government began to report to both the president and the legislature, but the legislature granted the president extraordinary powers, such as the right to issue decrees with the force of law and to impose martial law. Still not content, Gorbachev remade the government (council of ministers), this time supposedly on the US model, into a cabinet directly subordinated to the presidency. But then, in February–March 1991, he evicted the cabinet from the Kremlin to make way for his own presidential staff, whose departments were made to parallel the government ministries. In other words, the structure of the Soviet presidency—redundancy to the executive branch—reproduced that of the Central Committee apparat, which Gorbachev had only recently subverted.

Draining the CC apparat of its best functionaries, the Soviet presidential staff grew quickly.[1] But the president's ability to enforce decrees, and penalize non-compliance by the central and regional bureaucracy, remained elusive. Gorbachev had recreated the formal position of the general secretary in the presidency, but he had no substitutes for the bygone cult of the office of general secretary, the lost presence of Communist Party organizations throughout all institutions, or the cohesion once provided by Communist ideology and party 'discipline'. Vertical subordination was further undermined by the expropriations of state property, the assertiveness of republic legislatures, and the creation of republic presidencies. The Soviet state acquired a presidency suspended in the air, a government made redundant by the presidency, and members of a Soviet parliament expressing frustration at their decreasing ability to direct the president or the government. Following the failed August 1991 putsch by the marginalized cabinet, President Gorbachev dismissed his government and abolished the Supreme Soviet. Soon, of course, he, too, was gone.

Far from avoiding such self-defeating institutional arrangements, the Russian leadership under Yeltsin—obsessed with Gorbachev—*copied* them. First, Russia imitated the cumbersome model of a Congress of People's Deputies and separate working parliament (Supreme Soviet), the only one of the fifteen Union republics to do so. Then, Russia imitated the general-secretary-like presidency. But, whereas the Soviet legislature had acquiesced in the aggrandizement of the Soviet presidency, the Russian legislature, skilfully dominated by Yeltsin's hand-picked replacement as chairman, Ruslan Khasbulatov, dug in its heels. A twenty-month tug of war ensued, which seemed to turn on political programmes, since the president backed market liberalization, while the Supreme Soviet passed laws to increase industrial subsidies and pensions (without specifying how such measures would be financed, and having overwhelmingly endorsed shock therapy a few months before). The conflict also seemed to pivot on principle, since Yeltsin talked of overriding the Soviet-era Constitution still in force, while the parliament talked of defending it (though members did not hesitate to stockpile weapons). At bottom, the two sides were pursuing parallel quests for absolute supremacy.[2]

Amendments to Russia's Constitution confirmed the president as 'the highest official' (article 121) but designated the Congress as 'the highest organ of state power' (article 104).[3] Further ambiguity arose because the Russian Supreme Soviet—just like the direct democracy of Jacobin clubs, from which soviets (councils) were descended—incorporated both legislative and executive functions, while the Russian president enjoyed extra-parliamentary powers to issue decrees with the force of law, powers that after one year the parliament refused to renew. To break a stand-off that included impeachment efforts by the parliament and an April 1993 referendum won by the president—58 per cent expressed confidence in the president and 53 per cent in the painful economic reforms—Yeltsin issued an illegal decree in mid-September 1993 disbanding the two-tiered legislature, and calling for new elections as well as a referendum on a new Constitution. The leadership of parliament and their paramilitary supporters countered with an armed uprising, which ended in the presidential bombing and storming of the parliament building.[4] When the smoke cleared, the institutional settlements, like the clash itself, evoked Soviet and even tsarist legacies.

Yeltsin unilaterally promulgated a new 'presidential' Constitution, which was passed in a plebiscite. (When the preliminary voting results were reported to the president, he took a pen and raised the 'yes' vote from around 50 per cent to near 60 per cent.[5]) His Constitution re-established, but modified, the legislature, which now comprised a popularly elected lower house—the State Duma (a name from the tsarist period)—and an appointed upper house filled by regional officials from both the executive and the legislative branches—the Federation Council (a name evoking the Soviet era). But some ministers were no longer subjected to confirmation votes, and even the legislature's ability to confirm the prime minister was restricted by the fact that the president, like the tsar, could resubmit rejected candidates and, following three votes against confirmation, simply dismiss parliament. The Constitution also granted the Russian president, like the tsars and the politburo, permanent and nearly unrestricted power to issues decrees with the force of law—appropriating a prerogative of the legislature. For the executive branch, the president could issue binding orders, yet he also chastised the ministers (usually in front of television cameras), as if he were not responsible for his government's policies.

These arrangements were said to have been modelled on the French presidential–parliamentary hybrid, an outgrowth of France's monarchical traditions, but the

Russian president's formal powers far exceeded those of his French counterpart. Also unlike the French example, neither the Russian president nor the government he appointed had any moorings in parliamentary majorities.[6] Only one Russian prime minister, Yevgeny Primakov (September 1998–May 1999), forged a kind of coalition government—by voluntarily taking Duma deputies as ministers—but, after having brought a measure of equivocating stability, one day Primakov was summarily dismissed. (During two terms, Yeltsin sacked five prime ministers, around forty first deputy prime ministers, and more than 170 ministers overall.) Further unlike France, the Russian Constitution codified the practice whereby the 'force ministries' (the army, police, and renamed KGB) as well as the foreign ministry reported not to the prime minister, but to the president—as in Soviet times to the general secretary, and before that, to the tsar.

In a further reflection of autocratic traditions, Russia's presidency commanded a formidable bureaucracy of its own, whose departments paralleled and to an extent controlled the government ministries—just like the departments of Gorbachev's short-lived Soviet presidency had, and, before that, those of the CC apparat had. Appropriating the very premises of the old CC apparat, Yeltsin's Presidential Administration grew to have even more staff, spilling over into the Kremlin.[7] And in a new Property Office of the Presidential Administration, the Russian presidency acquired a financial base independent of the state budget that was even more phenomenal than those enjoyed by the tsars or the politburo. Amalgamating the three former property offices of the Central Committee, the Soviet Council of Ministers, and the Supreme Soviet legislature, Yeltsin's Presidential Property Office also expropriated or established more than 200 private businesses, from tourism and newspaper presses to construction and mineral extraction, with more than 100,000 total employees. It was the presidency, rather than the government or the legislature, that became the owner of Russian property abroad as well as of the Kremlin itself, Soviet-era elite hospitals, state-awarded vehicles, countless elite apartments, and the thousands of state dachas in or near Moscow, including those that were awarded to, or taken from, members of the legislature.

And yet, despite resources 'staggering in their scale and perplexity',[8] in the words of one scholar, the Russian president's effective power, like Gorbachev's, turned out to be highly circumscribed. Part of the reason was leadership, or the lack thereof. Yeltsin valued surprise over strategy in decision making, and suffered from severe mood swings and health problems, disappearing for long stretches without explanation. His presidency came to recall the latter years of Brezhnev's reign, when 'court' favourites enjoyed wide latitude because of the incapacitation of the 'tsar'.[9] But Yeltsin's enfeeblement was more than just a matter of poor health or personal quirks. It derived from the enigmatic political system. Defined as 'the guarantor of the constitution' (article 80), Russia's president did not govern; he was, like the tsar, a separate branch of government unto himself, the 'ruler' of those who governed. With the government detached from parliament and dependent on presidential whim, the duplicative Presidential Administration turned out to be less effective than even the CC apparat had been in overcoming the disconnected departmentalism of Russia's nearly 100 federal ministries and executive agencies.

Eighty-nine fiefs

As a part of the Union, Russia had been tied together by the centralized rule of the party and by the warring Moscow ministries that owned the major physical assets in localities. The sudden end of party rule and planned economy meant the onset, willy-nilly, of new centre–periphery relations. That prospect was further complicated by the same structural legacy that, as a result of Gorbachev's actions (and inactions), had made the Union vulnerable to separatism. The Russian republic, too, was a federation comprising, among its eighty-nine subunits, thirty-two nationally designated territories—either national republics or the lesser-status national districts. Several of Russia's national districts unilaterally raised themselves to the higher form, but only five of what came to be twenty-one national republics inside Russia had a majority of the titular nationality.[10] The country's population, over four-fifths Russian, was more ethnically homogenous than that of Spain or the UK. Russia's regional politics were shaped not by broad-based national movements, but by the formal existence of internal nation-state structures for largely unconcentrated minorities. By contrast, no 'autonomous republic' existed for the huge Russian populations concentrated in regions of Ukraine or Kazakhstan.

Watching the Union republics, including Russia, conduct insurgencies against Moscow, Russia's national and even non-national subunits began to assert the priority of their laws over federal ones. One republic in the Russian Federation, Chechnya, did more—it declared independence. In late 1991, Yeltsin decreed a state of emergency in Chechnya, but then immediately rescinded his order. Over the next several years, neither side displayed much wisdom or commitment to negotiations. Chechen gangsters—connected to Russian criminal groupings—engaged in local oil siphoning and hostage taking as well as international narcotics and weapons smuggling. Moscow conducted covert operations to destabilize the Chechen regime, with mixed results. In December 1994, the Russian army launched a frontal assault, despite a warning by the General Staff that a 'small victorious war', along the lines of the recent US intervention in Haiti, was impossible in Chechnya.[11] By mid-1996, after a brutal, disorganized military fiasco, Moscow sued for peace, leaving the status of Chechnya unresolved and ceding a free hand to the Chechen warlords. Neither Russian nor Chechen sovereignty offered much to the civilian population.

For all the drama of the Chechen War, which resumed in 1999, separatism was not the main challenge bedevilling Russia's federation.[12] Only one other republic, Tatarstan, also declared independence, but in February 1994—ten months before the onset of the Chechen War—the Tatar leadership signed a bilateral deal with Moscow renouncing its declaration in exchange for far-reaching autonomy and budgetary concessions from Moscow. Sakha (Yakutia), which had not pushed for independence, received much the same. Like Tatarstan, Sakha affirmed itself as part of Russia and achieved increased control over valuable resources on its territory, and its elites used these resources to consolidate their rule. Indeed, in all of Russia's internal republics, 'presidential' systems were created, so that Russia soon had twenty-one presidents, in addition to the federal president, and twenty-one extra presidential administrations (which were redundant to the government 'ministries' of the internal republics). Simultaneously, gubernatorial and mayoral bureaucracies expanded in Russia's fifty-seven non-ethnic provinces and federal cities.

Everywhere, an executive-branch aggrandizement took place, irrespective of whether regions were ruled by 'democrats' or Communists. In Krasnodar province, for example, old party elites lost scarcely a step after 1991 as a national-populist rose to power locally and maintained his position by doling out goodies and patronage. Tomsk province was convulsed by a strong democratic movement centred on the regional legislature, yet by 1994 pluralist politics had faded and the executive ran roughshod over the legislature. A similarly high-handed executive formed in Perm province, but they skipped the interlude of democratic movements and went directly to dividing the spoils of office. For Krasnodar, Perm, and even 'democratic' Tomsk, one scholar has persuasively argued, 'the re-establishment of executive dominance can be attributed to the continuation of old practices by incumbent politicians, by the weakness of the democratic opposition, or by presidential moves against [the federal legislature]'.[13] But in St Petersburg, 'democrats' dominated both the executive and the legislature. Yet the St Petersburg regional legislature never managed to operate effectively as policymaker.

That 'democratic' St Petersburg came to resemble 'Communist' Krasnodar suggested systemic factors at work. Across the country, one could trace a movement over the years 1989–94 of officials from high Communist Party posts first to elected regional soviets, then to the new regional executive bodies, which appropriated the local Soviet-era Communist Party headquarters sporting the best offices and communication equipment. This national trend could not be explained by the usual invocation of the baneful influence of Moscow's 'robber barons'. Nor could primary blame fall to the Kremlin, since the Kremlin was preoccupied with carrying out its own executive-branch aggrandizement at the federal level (as was Moscow's city government). Rather, the triumph of an executive-dominated, winner-take-all spoils system was rooted in the executive branch's manipulation of property, which was transferred to insiders connected to the executive or to members of the executive themselves. Regional legislatures busied themselves with acquiring 'their share' of the goodies distributed by the local executive.

What followed upon the loss of Communist Party and planned economy centralism was not so much 'decentralization', as many commentators suggested, as the formation of eighty-nine largely disconnected fiefs. Moscow's relations with the regions were semi-regulated by complicated budgetary politics and bilateral 'treaties', many of which, like local laws, contradicted the Federal Constitution. Branches of federal agencies—police, customs, tax collection—were dependent on regional bosses for offices, heat, salary supplements, and housing. Of course, regional barons and republic presidents did not completely control local property. But they used their office to confiscate revenue-generating businesses, subsidize friendly media, and choke off hostile media. Compelled to submit to elections, regional executives, especially in Russia's national republics, wielded powers over candidate registration, budget funds, and other means to block potential opponents. Many still lost re-election bids, but their successors often continued the flouting of federal laws. Kremlin pressure, and threats by President Putin to try to return the country to a system of centrally appointed regional leaders, did curb some of the most outlandish behaviour. But the Russian Federation—a product of the Soviet era, the Union's dissolution, and improvised bargaining—stood some way from becoming a functioning federation.

Towards the rule of law?

Alone among the Union republics, Russia did not have its own KGB—until May 1991, when one was established and given a handful of offices inside USSR KGB headquarters. After the August 1991 putsch, Yeltsin forced Gorbachev to appoint a person who would dismantle the Soviet KGB, but he simultaneously named a conservative career police official to run the incipient Russian KGB (which, though subdivided into foreign and domestic intelligence and variously renamed, was still colloquially known by its infamous Soviet-era acronym). At the time the Union was dissolved, the Russian KGB had grown by annexation from twenty-three officers to 20,000. Soon, it would expand to more than 100,000 and appropriate the USSR KGB's wealth of office buildings and other installations. This survival of the domestic arm of the KGB testified to Yeltsin's opportunism and political weakness: he had a mere dozen or so loyal clients, many from outside Moscow and thus lacking roots in the capital's deeply rooted, expansive patronage groups. It also testified to the undertow exerted by institutional legacies, and to the sheer number of Soviet state personnel that Russia inherited.

For the post-Soviet KGB, which still occupied the same armada of buildings in historic central Moscow, there were no more ideological nonconformists to persecute. Catching foreign spies was complicated by the fact that so many former and present KGB operatives were privately selling classified information, not all of it bogus. Anti-terrorist (and terrorist) operations claimed substantial man hours, but so did clandestine surveillance on the state elite, and the compilation of damaging dossiers on businessmen and politicians for cash. To spy on his staff and government, the Russian president formed his own mini-KGB, the Presidential Security Service (PSS), out of the former KGB directorate that had both protected and kept tabs on the Soviet elite.[14] The PSS also established a private firm, which specialized in the blackmail of the president's enemies and the assistance of court favourites. Yeltsin disbanded a rival 'parliamentary guard' that had been set up by a former first deputy chief of the USSR KGB, Filipp Bobkov, for Khasbulatov. But Bobkov then took numerous KGB operatives with him to a private media and financial company, MOST, which in effect acquired its own private KGB.[15] The gas monopoly, too, formed its own private KGB, as did many avowedly criminal groups.

Most KGB agents in private employ were either moon-lighters who retained their state posts or those who had left the agency yet remained in the 'active reserves'. What-ever the case, the fragmented organization's mystique and discipline were gone. What endured were many notorious practices, which—like other state 'services'—had become available to the highest bidder. Supposed transcripts of eavesdropped conversations among the high and mighty became a staple of Russian politics, yet these proved useful primarily for boosting newspaper circulation and

TV ratings. For attacking rival businessmen and politicians, a far more effective tool—also available for private hire and susceptible to political manipulation—was the new 40,000-strong tax police, whose power flowed from the rich ambiguities of Russia's prolific tax regulations and the lethal rates. Another handy weapon in political and commercial warfare turned out to be the state procurators and courts staffed by judges who, like the KGB operatives, were inherited from the Soviet Union.

No aspect of Russia's transformation was more overlooked or more important than legal reforms. Back in 1989, the 'Principles of the Law on Court Organization' passed by the USSR Supreme Soviet had established the presumption of innocence, a defendant's right to an attorney to combat coercion during confessions, and the introduction of jury trials to force prosecutors to prove accusations. But the Soviet Ministry of Justice, which controlled judges' wages and court budgets, aggressively subverted plans for the bureaucratic independence of the judiciary. So did the Soviet Procuracy, which was significantly larger and better financed than the court system, and had no parallel in a liberal order. Performing the functions of a public prosecutor, a procurator also had responsibility for 'overseeing legality', which meant the operation of the courts and state administration. The Procuracy, still lodged in its Soviet-era edifice, did little to ensure that the higher-ups in the executive branch behaved legally, yet it doggedly fought elimination of its power to supervise the courts.

Even before the end of the Union, Russia's Supreme Soviet adopted a 'Concept of Judicial Reform', outlining how Russian law and practice could be brought into line with international norms. The 'Concept' proposed establishing judicial control over the police, investigators, and procurator, institutionalizing the presumption of innocence as well as the right against self-incrimination, eliminating the accusatory functions of judges, and having trial by jury. A July 1993 'Law on Court Organization' enacted some of these goals, such as reviving jury trials (reintroduced, experimentally, in nine of Russia's eighty-nine regions). In addition, the 1993 Constitution reduced the scope of the Procuracy's jurisdiction, though, in a 1995 'Law on the Procuracy', the agency reacquired broad oversight powers over state administration. Also, whatever the law, many procurators simply skipped trials, leaving judges to interrogate defendants rather than act as neutral arbiters. Procurators even more than judges continued to wield vast formal powers on legal matters, though both groups were subjected to political pressure and, given their minuscule salaries, to financial inducement.[16]

A minority of high-level legal officials, guided by the view that Russia constituted a part of Europe, continued to provide impetus for legal reform—as had happened throughout modern Russian history. They struggled to have Russia's court system meet the new demands of a private-property, Constitutional order. The Soviet-era Supreme Court retained general jurisdiction over the law,

and higher courts continued a trend to show little defer-
ence to lower courts, issuing reversals even on findings of
fact.[17] But the Soviet system for settling commercial dis-
putes, state arbitrage (an underused administrative
agency), was remade into arbitrage courts, and, in
another innovation, a Constitutional Court was established (it was suspended by President Yeltsin in 1993–4,
and, when revived, its powers were curtailed, but it groped
its way towards issuing authoritative opinions on the
country's Basic Law[18]). The formation of this tripartite
judicial system was accompanied by a plethora of new
laws, and an increase in the number of legal professionals,
though these remained relatively few, to say nothing of
their quality. For example, the position of 'people's
assessors'—non-professionals who had ruled alongside
judges in the Soviet period—was eliminated, yet many
were drafted to serve as judges. Over the 1990s, Russia's
feeble population of judges nearly tripled from 6,000 to
around 17,000—giving the country still only one judge for
every seven or so KGB operatives.

Court funding, lacking a separate line item in the
federal budget, was haphazard and severely inadequate.
Judges, like most other federal officials (except the KGB),
became dependent on regional executives for housing,
heat, and everything else. The 1993 'presidential' Constitution afforded the president the power to nominate
judges for the high courts, and to appoint judges to all
federal courts, but the term 'federal' was not defined;
Boris Yeltsin took it to mean all courts in the Russian

Federation, but many regional leaders appointed local judges and even unilaterally restructured the judiciary on their territory. Plans to create inter-regional federal courts went unrealized. All of this reinforced the conspicuous disunity of the Russian Federation's legal space. Even Constitutional Court decisions could not be easily enforced outside Moscow—or inside, for that matter. Implementation of judicial decisions was a general problem, while decrees on combating organized crime granted security officials extraordinary powers of search and seizure that partially undermined the trend towards the protection of suspects' rights. Even many well-intentioned laws were very poorly written.

Inheriting Soviet institutional structures, and confronting difficult real-world challenges, Russian legal reform faced an uphill climb. The country experienced a great expansion of judicial jurisdiction, averaging in the mid- and late 1990s more than five million civil cases and well over one million criminal cases per year, yet many wronged parties sought redress not in the courts, where attorneys were necessary (and costly), but through free petitions to the local procurator, as in Soviet times, or through political connections. The 'demand' for law did not immediately follow upon its supply.[19] And yet, the greater role played by bribes, even the violent attacks on judges and court premises, perversely demonstrated the increasing importance of Russia's resource-poor, beleaguered legal machinery. Rather than functioning as a set of universally applicable and consistently enforced rules, the law in Russia remained a source of unpredict-ability, but further efforts at legal reforms were likely, driven partly by shifting business interests, and partly by a spreading practical desire to become competitive in the world economy.

Institutional kasha

Proponents of 'reform' inside and outside Russia, using self-serving categories such as 'democrat' (for themselves) and 'Communist' (for their enemies), obscured the fundamental issue of what happened to the remnants of the Soviet state. There was no mass emigration, no demolition of state office buildings—on the contrary, they were all packed to the hilt, and many underwent extension. Grandiose numbers of state personnel as well as long-established practices, even many entire agencies, endured the break-up. And, just as the nature of the collapse profoundly shaped the entire post-Soviet environment, so Soviet-era institutions and officials, as formidable 'facts on the ground', exerted immense influence on the scope and pace of any directed change. Of course, multiple new institutions were created. But, even when staffed by people with little or no experience in the Communist Party apparat or Soviet state, the new executive institutions bore the unmistakable stamp of the Soviet epoch, and even of the tsarist period.

Critics of 'reform' were right: Russia possessed its own

traditions. But their refrain that, by following the West's prescriptions Russia had ruined itself, mistook reformist rhetoric for institutional realities.[20] The critics, insisting that Russia should follow its own 'path', seem not to have noticed that, for the most part, Russia *did just that*. Critics also failed to make plain that, in an unsentimental world consisting of powerful countries with liberal systems, their 'defence' of Russia's institutional traditions condemned Russia's people to fall well short of their aspirations for prosperity. All cultures, not just Russia, are unique. Institutions differ markedly just within the G-7. But either a country has some form of an effective regulatory civil service, or it does not. Either a country has some version of a strong judiciary to enforce the rule of law, property rights, and the accountability of officials, or it does not. Either a country has a reliable banking system to make affordable credit available, or it does not. Russia did not. And the international power hierarchy (known as the world economy), making no allowances for culture, punished Russia for lacking efficacious variants of such institutions. Russia's entire economy ($350 billion) was valued at little more than total US health care fraud.

Russia's institutional landscape defied simple characterization. Democratic but not liberal, it had a constitutionally all-powerful president with limited effective power. Indeed Russia had more than twenty presidents. It had a boisterous parliament that often rhetorically pined for the days of Communism even though the Communist-era parliament had been a neutered lap dog. It had a federation without federal buildings in its regions and with regional executives sitting in the upper house of its Federal legislature (until they were kicked out in 2000 by Putin and the lower house). It had a grossly oversized KGB and a grossly undersized judicial system. It had a maze of laws that were not enforced and lacked some of the most elementary laws necessary for its new conditions. Its elites were under constant, illegal surveillance and only became more and more brazen. Its university law faculties became some of the most sought after in admissions, requiring—for those not gifted enough to pass on merit—among the highest illegal under-the-table payments. Its most corrupt politicians were among the loudest campaigners against corruption, while the constant decrying of corruption helped encourage the phenomenon, convincing officials that bribe taking was so ubiquitous there was no point in resisting.

Nowhere were the paradoxes of post-Soviet Russia more evident than in its media. Russia boasted very lively, professional media. Yet much of what appeared as 'news' in Russian media was paid for outright, infomercials camouflaged as reporting. Such cosiness might bring to mind American media dedicated to the entertainment industry, but, in Russia, commercial and political interests were able to purchase news column inches or news airtime to promote themselves and attack their enemies, with no acknowledgement of their sponsorship, in the same media that deftly and courageously exposed lies in government reports on the Chechen War, and financial scams tied to the politically powerful. Equally striking, the main 'private' television station, NTV, one of the country's foremost champions of a liberal, market order, took out loans for hundreds of millions of dollars and simply did not pay them back. When a complex combination of the gas monopoly and Putin's Kremlin forcibly pressed to have the loans paid, they seemed to be trying to eliminate one of their chief critics, rather than upholding the sanctity of contracts, but in fact the two pursuits could not be separated. Freedom of the press, like any other right, can be sustained only when it is adequately and properly financed.

Putin and much of the political establishment around him appeared much more receptive to problems of upholding shareholders' rights than human rights. That even Russia's best newspapers and TV stations yielded their integrity for cash and political expediency was widely known, but the country's media were still valued as indispensable to public life, and they were often the only source of reliable information available in the other former Soviet republics. Similarly, elections took place regularly, and, though subject to financial and political pressures, they were not rigged as in Belarus, Ukraine, Transcaucasia, or Central Asia. In Russia, the advent of democracy without liberalism had done much to reinforce the anti-liberal attributes and chaos of the state, but it also provided important political tools for reconstruction. Such was the contradictory, yet relatively less discouraging outcome of having to create new institutions when the main ingredients were Soviet institutions, and the country was not compelled to transform itself to qualify for entrance into the European Union. Ultimately, it was the Russian ambition to compete successfully against the liberal great powers that kept the issue of continued institutional change on the agenda.

Despite a multitude of changes, the post-Soviet social and political environment was littered by giant shards of old elites—a populous factory-director class with extensive inter-regional connections developed during the planned economy whose weight outweighed the over-hyped oligarchs affixed to the oil sector; a huge KGB and security establishment whose operatives often remained in close contact even if they moved to private 'security'; and an elephantine Moscow bureaucratic caste mirrored in regional executive bodies. As both the driving force and the debris of a debilitating imperial collapse, these elites lacked the old cohesion provided by ideology, an overarching organization, and an external threat, or new cohesion provided by strong, well-defined political parties or a clear-headed dialogue on the national interest, to say nothing of a sense of civic responsibility. A parade of patchwork 'anti-Communist' electoral coalitions, defined each time merely as the 'party of power', indicated the absence of effective organization. Entrenched in patronage groups, elites were only tenuously connected to the rest of society, which was itself disorganized.

The country was no longer a dictatorship, and had developed multiple and openly competitive sources of power. But too little of that infighting and contestation was regulated by the rule of law, and functionaries remained some distance from becoming a civil service. Uncertain and ongoing, Russia's predicament demonstrated a number of what should be self-evident truths. That civil society and a liberal state were not opposites but aspects of the same phenomenon. That government was not the enemy of liberty but its sine qua non. That private property without good government was not worth what it otherwise would have been. In short, that good government was the most precious thing a people could have. Russia's challenge was not cultural or economic but institutional, a problem of governability, especially of its governing institutions. This was the same challenge, in countless variations, across much of the contemporary world.

7

Idealism and treason

Despite oppression, despotism . . . and the privileges
of the ruling echelons, some of the people—and
especially the Communists—retain the illusions
contained in their slogans.

(Milovan Djilas, *The New Class,* 1957)

. . . the threat from Soviet forces, conventional and
strategic, from the Soviet drive for domination, from
the increase in espionage and state terror remains
great. This is reality. Closing our eyes will not make
reality disappear.

(US President Ronald Reagan, *Soviet Military
Power,* 1987)

For most of its history, the Russian empire was a highly
vulnerable great power striving for more than it could
achieve, ambitions that were a source of pride but also of
great misery. Under the stress of the First World War, the
empire disintegrated, yet most of its territory and its great-
power mission were revived in a new form, the USSR. The

Second World War brought the USSR deeper into Europe and Asia than Russia had ever been. But the system-against-system competition with the US and its allies strained the Soviet bloc—and its increasingly antiquated inter-war physical plant—to the breaking point, a circumstance acknowledged by Andropov and then Gorbachev, and cited by apologists for Ronald Reagan's military spending spree. Because the follow-on George Bush administration supposedly showed 'restraint' as the conquerors of Berlin initiated a humiliating retreat—and the Americans immediately began expanding NATO eastwards—those officials, too, awarded themselves high honours. The kudos was misappropriated. Gorbachev served up the severed head of his superpower on a silver platter and still had to employ all his artifice to cajole two US administrations to the banquet.[1]

Soviet socialism lost the competition with the world's most advanced countries, and could not have won even if it had spent far less on missiles and tanks. The crucial reasons for defeat were not the costly (for US taxpayers) fantasy of Star Wars (the KGB had sounded the alarm well before Reagan came along), but the crucial bipartisan resolve of containment, and, behind that, the Second World War victory over fascism and the post-war capitalist economic boom, consumer revolution, massive investments in social welfare, and decolonization. These momentous shifts meant that Soviet socialism could not provide a better standard of living, a more substantial safety net and just society, or a superior political order to that of the capitalist, welfare-state democracies. Of course, it was the USSR that lost more than twenty million lives to defeat Nazism. And it was the Soviet example that helped inspire, or frighten, groups in the West to push for the expansion of job programmes, unemployment benefits, pensions, medical subsidies, home mortgages, and public school lunches. And it was American cold-war hotheads who not only opposed the social welfare, but under the cover of 'national security' damaged the ultimate weapon of strength: open, accountable, democratic government.[2]

Just because it could not sustain the multidimensional global rivalry did not mean that the world's largest-ever police state—with a frightening track record of extreme violence—would suddenly liquidate itself, and, even more unexpectedly, do so with barely a whimper. In the 1980s, Soviet society was fully employed and the regime stable. The country had low foreign debt and an excellent credit rating. It suffered no serious civil disorders until it began to reform and even then retained the loyalty of its shrinking but still formidable Armed Forces, Ministry of Interior, and KGB. It was falling behind, but it could have attempted a retrenchment without the upheaval of perestroika. If unbearable competition with the US were the foremost concern that guided Soviet actions, why would the Soviet leader have exhausted himself trying to democratize the Communist Party? Why, having achieved deep disarmament, did he widen the political transformation and attempt to revive the radical-democratic system of soviets? Why, once it was clear that the survival of a centuries-old state was at stake, did the Soviet leader not employ the awesome force at his command and deliver a knock-out blow to the republican drives for independence? Because perestroika was not simply about global rivalry, but also about reclaiming the ideals of the October revolution.

Only in hindsight does the Soviet collapse appear predictable. The *simultaneous* demise of socialism and the USSR could have been foreseen only by someone who knew that socialism was born as non-capitalism and commanded allegiance, dependent on the image and realities of capitalism; that capitalism, and world geopolitics, had changed fundamentally from the inter-war to the post-Second World War period to the detriment of socialism; and that lifting censorship would make this evident. One also needed to know that the Soviet administrative structure, rather than being 'mono-organizational', was bifurcated into party and state; that the USSR was both a unitary state and a federation of national states that Moscow had helped foster; and that, although the Communist Party was redundant to state institutions, it was indispensable to the integrity of the Union. Above all, one needed to know that the October revolution was accompanied by deeply felt ideals, which endured all the nightmares, and that a quest to recapture those ideals would not only arise from within the system but, given the above-mentioned institutional arrangements, destroy it.

Astonishingly, perestroika accomplished what even the fantasists in the US national security establishment never dared to dream, and in the process made a dangerous early 1980s American brinksmanship look good.[3] What would the 'victorious' Americans have done, or would they even have been around, if the Soviet leadership had decided to utilize its immense war machine to hold power at all costs or to bring the world down with itself? And after 1991, what would subsequent US administrations have done if post-Soviet Russia had decided to profit, or wreak havoc, by transforming, say, Iran into a nuclear power on a par with France? Expand NATO into Romania? Both the causes behind the peaceful, surprise end of the cold war, and the geopolitics of the post-cold war, were poorly understood in Washington, whether under Republicans or Democrats.

Dissolved by its own ideals and elite

At Moscow University in the early 1950s, Gorbachev's Czech roommate, Zdeněk Mlynář, recalled of young Mikhail that, 'like everyone else at the time, he was a Stalinist', adding, shrewdly, that, 'in order to be a true reforming Communist, you have to have been a true Stalinist'. Mlynář should know: a former Stalinist, he went on to help draft, beginning in 1966, the Czechoslovak Communist Party's reformist 'Action Programme', which was published in April 1968. By then, Mlynář had become the chief ideologue of the Prague Spring, whose 'Action Programme' called for retaining the party's control while sanctioning a free press and competing associations—in short, something close to perestroika. Back in 1967, invited to explain Czechoslovakia's political reform plans in Moscow, Mlynář also paid a social visit to Gorbachev in Stavropol. The two talked of a renewed socialism devoid of Stalinist 'distortions', the enchanted fable for the educated, Marxist idealists of their cohort.[4] In fact, Lenin had not been less dictatorial or less ruthless than Stalin. But the myth that Lenin had been different, the myth of a redeemable party-led socialism, turned out to be of overriding importance. It had, in the post-Second World War conjuncture, the dissolving impact on Soviet structures that the First World War had on the then intact Habsburg state.

Gorbachev's ascent to the pinnacle of power in Moscow was not preordained, but neither was it a historical accident. It was a consequence of an inescapable generational change in the party leadership. Even Gorbachev's supreme tactical skills, so crucial for the full unfolding of perestroika, were not an accident, since such skills were a prime reason for his ascent as the top representative of his generation. Ligachev's timidity may also seem an accident, but he was elevated to the party's number two position by Gorbachev, who knew his deputy's weaknesses—and party history. Khrushchev's removal by the apparat, an event that helped motivate Gorbachev's 1988 sabotage of the party Secretariat, which unhinged the Union, was also not some happenstance. Under the pressure and logic of events, Khrushchev had brought forth the vision of a humanistic socialism as the party's answer to Stalinism, but his reforms resulted in his ouster. Khrushchev's sacking, and Brezhnev's caretaker reign, gave rise to the mistaken view that the key to Soviet politics was a struggle between 'reformers' and 'conservatives', a notion that misled Gorbachev as well as the voluminous commentary on him. The key was different: reform seemed necessary, but it would be tantamount to destabilization.

Those rare analysts, such as Vladimir Bukovsky, a dissident and then émigré, who did understand the Catch-22 nature of Soviet politics, predicted that, following a destabilizing reform, a system-saving crackdown would ensue, to be followed in future by another futile cycle of reform and reaction.[5] But Gorbachev proved Bukovsky wrong by not cracking down. Again, Mlynář provides the answer. In 1969, after Soviet tanks had crushed the Prague Spring, he was expelled from the party; eight years later, he joined a group of Czechoslovak intellectuals, artists, and former apparatchiks who initialled an appeal to the regime to uphold human rights—what became known as Charter 77. Mlynář had taken the next step in his evolution from committed Stalinist: discovering the impossibility of reforming socialism, he repudiated socialism, but he kept his humanist vision. That is also what happened to Gorbachev.[6] For him, amid the turmoil of perestroika, to have returned to Stalinist methods to preserve the system would have not only destroyed his international reputation but made a lie of his whole inner life. After 1991, Gorbachev remained a man of his convictions, recasting them as Western social democracy. The 'God that failed' had a leftist, not just a rightist, incarnation.

Only a few of Gorbachev's politburo colleagues shared his socialist romanticism, but even fewer matched his craftiness. He knew that opponents of his specific initiatives were not united and hesitated to demonstrate lack of confidence in the general secretary. Wielding the prestige of his office, he refrained from praising any politburo member in front of the rest, while making sure to convey his support for each in private. Outside the politburo, he knew that duty to party discipline inhibited his opponents from voting against proposals put forth in the party's name.[7] But perestroika was a party programme in more than name. For all his authority and hocus-pocus, Gorbachev could have got his way for so long only because everything he set out to do was within the framework of the revolution: raise industrial output's quantity and quality, advance peace, revitalize the Communist Party, activate the masses, reinvigorate the soviets. Only in 1990–1 did he begin, reluctantly, to discuss a possible market economy and the remaking of the Union, inducing party stalwarts to accuse him of being an agent of Washington.[8] But Gorbachev and his destabilizing quest for humane socialism had emerged from the soul of the Soviet system.

The October revolution's ideals—a world of abundance, social justice, and people's power—also informed Boris Yeltsin's anti-Communist populism (which used as its vehicle another fundamental element within the Soviet system: the republics). Glasnost revealed, for those still unaware, that the revolution's ideals were embedded in institutions that made them not only unrealized but also

unrealizable. Glasnost provoked outrage, because the
ideals were still powerful and people clung to them, in
their own ways. Of course, for many there were no ideals
to recapture, just a system to overthrow (the very few dissidents) or to perpetuate (the many 'patriots'). But anyone
who spent time in the USSR during the late 1980s and
early 1990s knows just how passionately hopeful much of
the heartland was. It was an ambivalent hope, full of scep-
ticism, and rooted in a visceral separation of the Communist Party from Soviet (people's) power and justice.
This is what Gorbachev tapped during the 1989 Congress
of People's Deputies that riveted the country. Then,
Yeltsin came along and brought the promise of the ideals
without the party and apparatchiks! The people, and some
suddenly former party members, embraced him as they
had embraced no one else.

When Yeltsin launched his populist crusade he was
probably no less sincere than Gorbachev had been, but it
was obvious Yeltsin had less of a sense of post-Communism
than Gorbachev had had of the structural booby traps
of the old system. Attempting to rule Moscow, let alone
Russia, with a tiny group of self-styled 'democrats', some
cronies from the Urals, and other administrative in-
competents brought a rude awakening. Yeltsin quickly
became a willing vehicle for the human detritus of the
Soviet-era institutions that had smothered the revolutionary ideals and had been stirred by Gorbachev's efforts to
bring them to life. True, the vast elite underwent transformation, yet most of it survived, especially the upwardly

mobile second and third echelons. At the same time, freed from Communist Party 'discipline' and legitimated by elections, office-holders became far more venal than they or their predecessors had been when Yuri Andropov had begun assembling a team of earnest apparatchiks, headed by Gorbachev, to combat official corruption. The acclaim, and then loathing, for Yeltsin afforded further evidence that long-held dreams for a better, more just world were structures in the Soviet socio-political landscape, and the main chemical agent in the system's unexpected, relatively peaceful dissolution.

China offered an important counterpoint. Many people regretted that Gorbachev had not followed the Chinese model of reforms. Under Deng, the Chinese leadership *bolstered* the party's monopoly by allowing—at first grudgingly—market behaviour to flourish, while maintaining political controls with repression. But China did not have to overcome the wreckage of the world's largest ever assemblage of obsolete equipment. Heavy industry in China was in deplorable shape, yet the population was 80 per cent peasant. Also, China's economic boom was made possible by massive direct foreign investments, some $300 billion in the 1990s, mostly from overseas Chinese (and secondarily Japanese and American investors); Russia had no Hong Kong or Taiwan. Finally, the ambiguous results in China—the widespread unpaid debts, the unsecured property rights, the official malfeasance—were not necessarily so different from those in Russia. And the Chinese process was far from over.[9] Be that as it may, China's example was further proof that socialism with a human face precipitated the Soviet collapse. Instead of a Deng or Beria-type ruthless pragmatist, Soviet reforms were carried out by someone willing to sacrifice centralized power in the name of party democracy but hesitant for ideological reasons to support full-bore capitalism—in short, by a Khrushchevian true-believer.

The armageddon that never was

Academic Russia watchers, formerly known as Sovietologists, survived the collapse. Prior to 1991, one side (the left) had staked its reputation on the argument that a reform group would materialize and change the system, perhaps making it democratic; the other (the right) had insisted that the system was incapable of reform. Since Soviet socialism *proved to be* unreformable *and* Gorbachev the reformer presided over the system's docile replacement by a democratically elected government, each side refused to concede defeat, a boldness backed by tenure. Both were wrong. Neither had a clue about the institutional dynamic that tied the fate of the Union to the fate of socialism—the party's simultaneous redundancy and indispensability to the federal Soviet state. The right's realism about the Soviet system's coercion and insoluble contradictions was wilfully blind to the elements of popular consent and positive content in the revolution's enduring ideals, which were crucial for converting reform into repudiation. The left's romanticism about a reform that would make socialism humane was, as the right argued, an illusion, but this illusion sustained what the right thought impossible—the top-down, self-dismantling of the system.

How many Sovietologists understood the depth of Gorbachev's reform-socialist beliefs, the mortal danger they posed to the system, and their likely evolution, foreshadowed by Mlynář (and many others), into a humanist repudiation of Leninism? Who appreciated the profound gulf between the seemingly similar 'conservative' number two men—Mikhail Suslov, who helped orchestrate the palace coup against Khrushchev, and Yegor Ligachev, who never moved to oust Gorbachev yet drew so much miscomprehending attention? Which analysts understood that the republics, especially the Russian republic, could be vehicles to power for ambitious members of the middle echelon and irresistible safe harbours for the drifting, well-armed top elites? Russia as a refuge from the Union! Who recognized that unconstrained access to state-owned property and state bank accounts would turn elite betrayal, unintentionally augmented by Gorbachev's renewal efforts, into a mass movement? Idealism unleashing the basest opportunism? There was a Shakespearian quality to the system's surprise, yet ultimately logical self-destruction, inaugurated by romanticism and consummated by treason.

A fortunate blend of fair and foul, of principled restraint and scheming self-interest, brought a deadly system to meek dissolution. No republic branch of the KGB broke openly from the Union until early August 1991, when the Georgian KGB proclaimed its allegiance to the Georgian president.[10] Interior ministry police troops—about 350,000 strong—were becoming more dependent on local authorities for resources, but they were also undergoing deepened militarization at Moscow's direction.[11] As for the army, republics were assuming greater responsibility for the draft and conscripts were increasingly serving on the territory of their home republic, but 'somewhat surprisingly', a top expert concluded, the Armed Forces 'did not collapse overnight. The major command structures proved fairly resilient.'[12] Thankfully, however, reform socialism meant breaking with anything that resembled Stalinism or Brezhnevism, including domestic military crackdowns; even the men who belatedly attempted in August 1991 to salvage the Union chose not to mobilize more than a tiny fraction of their available might, which in any case they failed to use. In this light, perestroika should be judged a stunning success.[13] Reform socialism also, unintentionally, incited Soviet elites to tear their system apart, which they did with gusto. In this light, too, perestroika was a success.

Remember the mesmerizing maps of Eurasia covered with miniature tanks, missile launchers, and troops representing the Soviet military that appeared on American television for Congressional debates over Pentagon appropriations? This hyper-militarized USSR, during the troubles of perestroika, did not even *attempt* to stage a cynical foreign war to rally support for the regime. Remember the uproar over Saddam Hussein's August 1990 invasion of Kuwait—right amid the Soviet drama—and his feared possession of weapons of mass destruction? Iraq's capabilities were trivial next to the Soviet Union's. Remember the decades of cold-war warnings, right through the 1980s, about the danger of a pre-emptive Soviet first strike? Even if Soviet leaders had calculated that they were doomed, they could have wreaked terrifying havoc out of spite, or engaged in blackmail. Remember the celebrated treatises equating the Soviet and Nazi regimes? The Nazi regime, which never acquired atomic weapons, held on to the last drop of blood. Remember the wrath that Franklin Roosevelt incurred for 'handing over' Eastern Europe to Stalin at Yalta? Roosevelt had not a single soldier on the ground. Gorbachev had 500,000 troops in Eastern Europe, including 200,000 in Germany *after* the unification. The Warsaw Pact command and control structure remained operational right through the end of 1991.

It was Gorbachev who 'handed over' Eastern Europe. Flabbergasted by events, he turned over the jewel in Moscow's crown, Berlin, which had been paid for with the highest price in lives world history has yet seen, and in return he got some cash and credits, soon to be wasted, as well as empty promises of partnership. At a 1994 ceremony to mark the completion of troop withdrawals, Boris Yeltsin, in a depressed, drunken state, grabbed a baton and started conducting a German orchestra, causing a scandal. How much worse it all might have turned out, if a strong leader and faction of the Moscow elite had shown ruthless determination to uphold the empire, or, even after the situation had ceased to be salvageable, had indulged in malice or lunacy. Much had changed in the world since the 1940s, but the bloodbath of Yugoslavia's demise in the 1990s certainly gives pause. Historically, such a profoundly submissive capitulation, as took place in the Soviet case, was a rarity.[14]

Less 'reform' than ongoing collapse

The complacency attending the Soviet collapse was matched only by the chutzpah among outsiders, such as officials of the Reagan and (first) Bush administrations, in pirating credit for it. And outsiders' arrogance only grew in relation to post-Soviet Russia. President Clinton's Administration awarded itself a prominent role in guiding the Russian 'transition'. But this characteristically American self-promotion, which involved relentless 'pro-consul' visits to Moscow, soon became embarrassing. Eventually, even the White House began to understand that Russia would not become a liberal polity or secure market economy overnight. 'Blame' for Russia's 'failure' was craftily shifted to the International Monetary Fund (whose organizational chart had the US Treasury Secretary at the top). The IMF had much to answer for, of course, but the more important point was that the role of Washington and the outside world—during both the 'credit' and the 'blame' phases—was absurdly exaggerated. Mostly, the self-assigned role of the West in 'promoting' but not financing with direct investments Russia's 'transition' had the effect of empowering anti-Western sentiment inside Russia, and anti-Russian sentiment in the West.

Russia's reform conundrum, beyond achieving a difficult macroeconomic stabilization, entailed the need to create altogether new state capacity, including the rootedness of the state in organized social constituencies and individuals' identities, when a massive and dysfunctional anti-liberal state, alongside a non-market and time-warp economy, was the chief inheritance from the USSR. That is why, at the most basic level, Russia did not undergo sustained liberal reform; it was simply not possible, given the social and institutional landscape inherited from the Soviet period, as well as the loss of the limited constraints that had been in place on state officials. The discourse of 'neo-liberal reform', which presupposed near complete extirpation of the Soviet era, did have the effect of moving political battles (and to an extent, socio-economic structures) more quickly to the question of the proper forms, rather than the very existence, of private property and the market. Of course, 'reform' also galvanized initially disoriented, and very large, Soviet-era interest groups. Raising expectations wildly proved to be a self-defeating endeavour. Ultimately, it was 'reform', rather than the Soviet inheritance, that took the blame for the country's lingering woes. At the same time, however, the 1990s cannibalization of the Soviet era amounted to a kind of 'reform', imparting some severe lessons and painfully opening the way for new, albeit still circumscribed, possibilities.

To put the matter another way, the Soviet collapse *was* a collapse, rather than an overthrow (as in Poland), and, in post-Soviet Russia, the collapse continued.[15] Outside a rich and spectacularly renovated Moscow, and cities in Moscow's orbit, the slide proceeded apace throughout the 1990s. Long-distance trains and urban mass-transit systems still functioned, but Soviet-era hospitals and schools were decaying or closing, while power grids were ageing and not being replaced. In more remote areas, Soviet-built airports were overgrown with weeds and riverboats rusted along once popular routes to dilapidated summer camps. Russia's Soviet-era prison complexes, bulging with over one million inmates at any given time (more than in the entire Soviet Union during its last decade), had to handle up to five million detainees who passed through the system annually, at least 100,000 of whom suffered from drug-resistant diseases, which spread to the rest of society. Alcoholism, which also did not begin in 1991, affected up to twenty million Russians, one-seventh of the population. Life expectancy at birth was in decline (essentially since the 1970s), and the population was shrinking. Untreated toxic wastes continued to flow into contaminated rivers and water tables. 'No other great industrial civilization so systematically and so long poisoned its land, air, water, and people,' two analysts wrote of the Soviet Union, adding of Russia that 'no advanced society faced such a bleak political and economic reckoning with so few resources to invest toward recovery'.[16]

Doubtless the most spectacular dimension of the collapse was the disintegration of the world's largest-ever military—as if the old televised maps depicting Soviet capabilities had been a mirage. The Union's break-up was one cause of the military's crumbling: many systems, such as Soviet-era radar and air defence systems, were largely unsalvageable, since they were integrated structures with indispensable parts spread in different republics. Lack of money was equally responsible. In 1989, the USSR built seventy-eight submarines and ships; a decade later, Russia built four, one of which, the Kursk, blew itself up and sank. Almost all the weapons still produced by the radically downsized military-industrial-complex were for export, since foreign customers paid for deliveries. Much of even the intact equipment Russia inherited from the Soviet period had to be abandoned for want of spare parts and maintenance. Suddenly, Sweden's navy was estimated to have three times the strength of Russia in the Baltic Sea, and Turkey twice the strength of Russia in the Black Sea. In the Far East, the Russian navy essentially ceased to exist, rusting in port. In ground forces, Russia inherited 186 Soviet divisions, about two-thirds the number that had existed back in 1985, but by 1996 Russia had just thirty divisions—on paper. At most ten were battle ready. Security issues, like the environmental and health quagmire, were as pressing as political and economic changes. Meanwhile, police troops of the Interior Ministry had ballooned to twenty-nine divisions, and the tax police as well as the new Emergency Ministry personnel were militarized, like US SWAT teams, as if Russia were fighting a society-wide domestic war.

While Soviet-era buildings housing the ministry of defence and the General Staff were jammed to capacity by members of the still immense military establishment, army conscripts were fed dog food, and sadistic hazing became so violent that commanding officers stopped going near the barracks; anyway, who had time to supervise troops when shovelling manure on the side to feed one's family? Desertions and evasions of call-ups numbered in the tens of thousands. In 2000, President Putin, who had begun a career in the KGB right when it had started secretly warning of the country's nosedive, and whose subsequent life experience had revolved around the failure to institutionalize market capitalism in St Petersburg, promised to arrest and possibly even reverse Russia's decline. Perhaps he would succeed—he did manage an important tax overhaul in 2000, creating incentives for business activity and transparency. But that same year, having worked over many months trying to sort out infighting among the top brass over the direction of military 'reforms', he announced that troop strength would be cut from 1.2 million to 800,000, even though the mobilization for the second Chechen War (in 1999) had turned up well under 100,000 grunts, so that 'contract fighters' had to be hired. Putin's spokesman then rescinded even the announcement that reductions of non-existent troops had been agreed to by the generals. Crucial military 'reform', in other words, was a lot like 1990s economic 'reform': a mixture of breast beating over what needed to be done, all-out resistance to common-sense initiatives, and embezzlement of what allocations were made.

News reports, meanwhile, of interdicted nuclear smuggling (exclusively from civilian sites), missile command posts disrupted by 'entrepreneurs' prospecting for the marketable copper contained in cables, and strategic rocket forces staging strikes over wage delays demonstrated over and over that this was no ordinary collapse. It would be better for all concerned if Russia had professional, disciplined armed forces that could guarantee its security and reliable control over its weapon stockpiles, including approximately 1,300 tons of highly enriched uranium as well as between 150–200 tons of plutonium. (Around eight kilograms are sufficient for a bomb.) Weapons elimination or secure storage was, far-sightedly, being funded by the US, but only partially.[17] Russia also had the world's largest assemblage of chemical weapons, 44,000 metric tons. (A single phial of sarin gas caused terror in the Tokyo subway.) In 1993 Moscow signed the Chemical Weapons Convention, which the Duma ratified in 1997, agreeing to destroy its arsenal within ten years (with a possible five-year extension), but finances remained a pipe dream.[18] Finally, Russia had plenty of experts who knew how to manufacture biological weapons.[19] In fact, its tens of thousands of nuclear, chemical, and biological weapons scientists and technicians, acting with or without the government's blessing, could have altered the strategic balance of any world region. 'Only the intense pride and patriotism of Russian nuclear experts has prevented a proliferation catastrophe', concluded a team of concerned scientists, who added that, 'virtually everything else in Russia is for sale'.[20]

Whither Russia? Eurasia. But whither the world?

In 1983, one perceptive scholar, surveying the hollowing of Communist ideology, predicted that Russian nationalism 'could become the ruling ideology of state'.[21] A decade later, warnings about nationalism became highly fashionable. But such warnings went unfulfilled. To be sure, Boris Yeltsin had sought to rally liberal nationalists with his campaign for Russia's rebirth, which, however, turned out to be more collapse. Hardline nationalists drifted toward the re-established, ageing Communist Party, whose cynical leader, Gennady Zyuganov, had conveniently been away 'on vacation' when the president bombed the parliament in October 1993, and returned to fill the void in the 'opposition'. A chauvinistic grouping, led by the media clown Vladimir Zhrinovsky, also garnered a limited protest vote, for a time, while a handful of avowedly fascist associations, some affiliated with the re-constituted Communists, engaged in sporadic acts of violence, most of which went unpunished. But the pundits, mesmerized by rhetoric and confusing the existence of chaos with the possible onset of powerful dictatorship, were wrong: the much-feared red–brown (Communist–fascist) coalition failed to materialize. Chauvinistic nationalism, as well as a potentially helpful liberal nationalism, remained weak, disorganized political forces in Russia. When Leninism committed suicide, essentially nothing took its place. Except 'transition' and 'reform'.

Palpable regret over the dissolution of the Union did not signify a desire, generally understood to be futile, to bring the past back. But because the 'greatness of Russia' had been fused with Communist ideology, a colossal void opened. In 2000, Russia was still without words to its post-Soviet national anthem. President Putin agreed to bring back the Soviet-era anthem, for which new words were written. The music had first been introduced in 1943, and provided inspiration in the war against Nazi Germany. Putin also brought back the red Soviet flag—but only for the Russian army, and without the hammer and sickle. The red flag had flown over the captured Nazi Reichstag in 1945. That defining episode in Russia's climactic history, in many ways the pivot of the twentieth century, was emotionally what endured from the Communist epoch. For fascism to come to power in Russia, it had much to overcome psychologically, never mind that millions of stormtroopers or squadristi were nowhere on the horizon, and that the populace, still though generally unburdened of Soviet ways of speaking, wanted what it had desired before perestroika began: a mixed economy, political liberalization with limits, and a state that ensured public order and some measure of social justice.

Only five countries, which were already better off and which were close to and willingly emulated Germany/ Austria or Scandinavia—Slovenia, Hungary, the Czech Republic, Poland, and Estonia—managed a first rush of liberal reform, and were poised for a second push (greatly aided by European Union accession and its requirement of institutional 'harmonization').[22] Even the touted cases of Latvia and Lithuania resembled the disasters of Ukraine and Belarus (both partially subsidized by Russia), though the Caucasus and Central Asia were still worse in their economic and political involution. The one exception of comparative well-being in the East was the city of Moscow and its surrounding region, whose population and wealth exceeded that of all the (relatively) successful countries except Poland. Thus, Russia was struggling, but it had a megalopolis whose extraordinary concentration of talent and material resources helped partly compensate for institutional shortcomings. And, relative to its immediate neighbours, Russia was in far better shape, a very sad commentary on the others. Indeed, on the eve of the tenth anniversary of the collapse, the cheering for the end of the Union had given way in a majority of former Soviet republics to sober reflection. But circumstances had dictated that the Union, minus the three Baltic states, could not have been saved, in order to be transformed, without substantial bloodshed.

The modern world is not a democracy of nations but a

hierarchy, as anyone whose country is not among the richest and most powerful could readily attest. Only breathtaking naïvety allowed both Gorbachev and Yeltsin to assume that Moscow would be admitted to the elite club of nations out of sympathy, or on its own terms. Putin seems more sanguine, harbouring no illusions about 'partnership' with the US and identifying Russia's interests, properly, with Europe, though not at the expense of its interests (and former markets) in Asia, from Iraq and Iran to India, China, and the Korean peninsula. The problem is that Russia is generally outside processes of world integration. Of the world's three main blocs, two of which partially overlap security systems, and all three of which have the US as a centrepiece—NAFTA; Pacific Rim/US–Japan Alliance; European Union/NATO—Russia has no prospect of joining any. But, even though it is geographically farther from the heart of Europe than at any time since the eighteenth century—with the exception of its Kaliningrad enclave—Russia's best hope, as a great power and a dignified country, is probably to try to join the euro.

Russia's future also entails some kind of reintegration within its own potential NAFTA, the phantom CIS. As in the aftermath of the British and French colonial empires, or the aftermath of the Japanese and German wartime systems, Russia—given its size, capabilities, and energy resources—could be expected to maintain a position of diplomatic and economic strength in lands it used to rule. By world standards, that would not be a return to imperialism, but an expression of what is usually called the power of the market. But whether, in the meantime, the present world economy under US hegemony would go the way of the first—the late-nineteenth-century one under British imperial hegemony—remains to be seen.

No one knows the future, of course, but every historian knows that the current conjuncture will change. Nineteenth-century Britain, whose vast commercial and geopolitical empire was mind-boggling, had refused to tolerate the abrupt rise of German power on the continent, especially German ambitions to build a navy beginning in 1898. Sucking in all the great powers on either side of the Anglo-German rivalry, the First World War and its consequences, including fascism, Nazism, Soviet socialism, and the Great Depression, ended the first world economy and culminated in the Second World War, which brought even greater death and devastation. But that war also ushered in a second world economy with a new, and differently organized, commercial and geopolitical empire—the United States.[23]

Only the Soviet Union, among the great powers, had been defiantly out of step with the changes wrought by the Second World War and the dominance of the basic US model, but in 1991 the Soviet outlier came crashing down peacefully. This turn of events may have exposed, and even helped unloose, the instability inherent in the second world economy. Capitalism is an extremely dynamic source of endless creation, but also of destruction. Interconnections bring greater overall wealth but also heightened risks. And the US—bearing a titanic national security establishment not demobilized after the cold war, exhibiting a combustible mixture of arrogance and paranoia in response to perceived challenges to its global pretensions, and perversely disparaging of the very government institutions that provide its strength—makes for an additional wild card.

Notes

1. History's cruel tricks

1 Daniel Yergin, *The Prize: The Epic Quest for Oil, Money, and Power* (New York, 1991), 588–673.

2 Geoffrey Tweedle, *Steel City: Entrepreneurship, Strategy, and Technology in Sheffield, 1743–1993* (Oxford, 1995), 1–7.

3 Companies cut line workers at a far higher rate than costlier, better-paid managers. David M. Gordon, *Fat and Mean: The Corporate Squeezing of America and the Myth of Managerial 'Downsizing'* (New York, 1996).

4 Terry F. Buss and F. Stevens Redburn, *Shutdown at Youngstown: Public Policy for Mass Unemployment* (Albany, NY, 1983), 4. See also John Strohmeyer, *Crisis in Bethlehem: Big Steel's Struggle to Survive* (Bethesda, MD, 1986), 11–14; Barry Bluestone and Bennet Harrison, *The Deindustrialization of America* (New York, 1982); and Lloyd Rodwin and Hidehiko Sazanami (eds.), *Deindustrialization and Regional Economic Transformation: The Experience of the United States* (Boston, 1989).

5 Michael J. Piore and Charles F. Sabel, *The Second Industrial Divide: Possibilities for Prosperity* (New York, 1984); Philip Cooke (ed.), *The Rise of the Rustbelt* (London, 1995).

6 Quoted in William E. Schmidt, 'A Steel City Still Needs Help Despite Big Steel's Comeback', *New York Times*, 4 Sept. 1989. Another flagship of US Steel (now USX), the Homestead Works, employed 20,000 workers in 1945, 9,000 in

the 1970s, 3,500 in the early 1980s, and 23 the day the mill closed in July 1986. Immediately after the Second World War, about 40% of all wage-earners in the US had owed their livelihood directly or indirectly to the steel industry.

7   John Brant, 'Unemployment: The Theme Park', *New York Times Magazine*, 28 Jan. 1996. On a similar coke-oven theme park in Germany, see Alan Cowell, 'Old German Steel Plant Becoming a Tourist Site', *New York Times*, 17 Dec. 1995. Originally, the plans for Johnstown had called for creating a fully-fledged national park, with old-style pubs and restored company housing, to showcase a working-class community. That never happened.

8   Henry Kissinger, *Years of Upheaval* (Boston, 1982), 854.

9   Heinrich Hassmann, *Oil in the Soviet Union: History, Geography, Problems* (Princeton, 1953), 109; Robert W. Campbell, *Trends in the Soviet Oil and Gas Industry* (Baltimore and London, 1976).

10   Thane Gustafson, *Crisis amid Plenty: The Politics of Soviet Energy under Brezhnev and Gorbachev* (Princeton, 1989), 47.

11   Khrushchev is also recorded as having said, 'There are people in the Soviet Union who would say that as long as Stalin was in command, everyone obeyed and there were no great shocks, but now [these new bastards] have come to power, Russia has suffered the defeat and loss of Hungary' (Mark Kramer, 'The Soviet Union and the 1956 Crises in Hungary and Poland: Reassessments and New Findings', *Journal of Contemporary History*, 33/2 (1998), 163–214 (at 173, 191).

12   Charles S. Maier, *Dissolution: The Crisis of Communism and the End of East Germany* (Princeton, 1997); Roman Laba, *The Roots of Solidarity: A Political Sociology of Poland's Working-Class*

Democratization (Princeton, 1991); Martin Malia, 'Poland: The Winter War' and 'Poland's Eternal Return', *New York Review of Books*, 18 Mar. 1982 and 29 Sept.1983. See also Kazimierz Z. Poznański, *Poland's Protracted Transition: Institutional Change and Economic Growth 1970–1994* (New York, 1996). In the 1970s, Polish economists began to ponder how socialist planning, which presupposed autarky, could be carried out if Poland were to become more and more tied to the world economy. See the (accidentally) prescient work by Marian Ostrowski and Zbigniew Sadowski, *Wyzwania rozwojowe* (Warsaw, 1978).

13 Robert M. Gates, *From the Shadows: The Ultimate Insider's Story of Five Presidents and how they Won the Cold War* (New York, 1996), 89; Nikolai Leonov, *Likholet'e* (Moscow, 1995), 164–5; Pavel Palazchenko, *My Years with Gorbachev and Shevardnadze: The Memoir of a Soviet Interpreter* (University Park, PA, 1997), 24.

14 Fred Halliday, 'A Singular Collapse: The Soviet Union, Market Pressure and Inter-State Competition', *Contention*, 1/2 (1992), 121–41.

15 Konstantin Simis, *USSR: The Corrupt Society: The Secret World of Soviet Capitalism* (New York, 1982), 248.

16 William A. Clark, *Crime and Punishment in Soviet Officialdom: Combating Corruption in the Political Elite 1965–1990* (Armonk, NY, 1993); T. H. Rigby, 'A Conceptual Approach to Authority, Power, and Policy in the Soviet Union', in Rigby *et al.* (eds.), *Authority, Power, and Policy in the USSR: Essays Dedicated to Leonard Schapiro* (London and Basingstoke, 1983), 9–31.

2. Reviving the dream

1 Peter Gornev [pseudonym], 'The Life of a Soviet Soldier', in Louis Fischer (ed.), *Thirteen Who Fled* (New York, 1949), 39. On the process of Soviet defection, including the centrality of knowledge of the outside world, see Jay Bergman, 'The Memoirs of Soviet Defectors: Are They a Reliable Source about the Soviet Union?', *Canadian Slavonic Papers*, 31/1 (1989), 1–24.

2 Richard Crossman (ed.), *The God that Failed* (New York, 1950), which contains the stories of six prominent Communist apostates, including the editor of the anthology with Gornev's story. Many former Communists did indeed become anti-Communists on the right. But there was another path, the path traced by Mikhail Gorbachev and millions of others, as my narrative develops.

3 Elena Zubkova, *Russia after the War: Hopes, Illusions, and Disappointments, 1945–1957* (Armonk, NY, 1998), 91–2.

4 Mikhail Gorbachev, *Memoirs* (New York, 1996), 60. See also Archie Brown, *The Gorbachev Factor* (New York, 1996). On the Stavropol days, see the exposé by Boris Kuchmaev, *Otverzhennyi s bozh'ei otmetinoi: Tainoe i iavnoe v zhizni Mikhaila Gorbacheva*, 2nd edn. (Stavropol, 1992); and the bitter reminiscences of Anatolii A. Korobeinikov, *Gorbachev: Drugoe litso* (Moscow, 1996).

5 Nikolai Leonov, *Likholet'e* (Moscow, 1995), 47–55. Leonov describes being swept off his feet by meeting Raul Castro and Che Guevarra. Oleg Kalugin, another young KGB officer, who went as an exchange student to Columbia University in 1958, recalls romantic reactions to the Khrushchev era and sincere party beliefs, which were also very close to Gorbachev's. Kalugin with Fen Montaigne, *The First*

Directorate: My 32 Years in Intelligence and Espionage against the West (New York, 1994).

6 The blueprint for a Communist future resembled a much-expanded welfare state. Sergei Strumilin, 'Mir cherez 20 let', *Kommunist*, 13 (1961), 25–36. A transition to Communism was first announced in 1947–8, but quickly dropped. Zubkova, *Russia after the War*, 141.

7 Gorbachev, *Memoirs*, 102.

8 Valery Boldin, *Ten Years that Shook the World: The Gorbachev Era as Witnessed by his Chief of Staff* (New York, 1994), 175–6. Gorbachev graciously writes (*Memoirs*, 97) that Kulakov, an important patron, died of heart failure, the officially reported cause of death (*Pravda*, 18 July 1978). The other leading contender to replace Kulakov, Sergei Medunov of agricultural Krasnodar, had known Brezhnev since the war, but was tarnished by corruption charges leaked by Andropov's KGB. Arkady Vaksberg, *The Soviet Mafia: A Shocking Exposé* (New York, 1991). On Kulakov see Zhores A. Medvedev, *Gorbachev* (New York, 1986), 76–7, 87–93, and Seweryn Bialer, *Stalin's Successors: Leadership, Stability, and Change in the Soviet Union* (New York, 1980), 76–7.

9 Public abandonment of the 'final transition' came only in February 1981, after much gnashing of teeth over 'depriving' the Soviet people of the possibility of achieving Communism. Vadim Pechenev, *Gorbachev: K vershinam vlasti* (Moscow, 1991) 21, 48.

10 Donna Bahry, 'Society Transformed? Rethinking the Social Roots of Perestroika', *Slavic Review*, 52/3 (1993), 512–14.

11 Filipp Bobkov, *KGB i vlast'* (Moscow, 1995), 242.

12 Dmitri Volkogonov, *Autopsy for an Empire: The Seven Leaders who Built the Soviet Regime* (New York, 1998), 313–15;

Mikhail Dokuchaev, *Moskova. Kreml'. Okhrana* (Moscow, 1995), 102. In ten years under Khrushchev, there were eleven uprisings involving 300 or more people, and during the eighteen years of Brezhnev's rule only nine more, mostly over price hikes, living conditions, or ethnic grievances. The authorities repressed 'ringleaders', enforced news blackouts, and held pre-emptory conversations with anyone aware of the events. Vladimir A. Kozlov, *Massovye besporiadki v SSSR pri Khrushcheve i Brezhneve (1953—nachalo 1980-x gg.)* (Novosibirsk, 1999); 'O massovykh besporiadkakh c 1957 goda', *Istochnik*, 6 (1995),146–53.

13 Ludmilla Alexeyeva, *Soviet Dissent: Contemporary Movements for National, Religious, and Human Rights* (Middletown, CT, 1985), 449.

14 Yitzhak M. Brudny, *Reinventing Russia: Russian Nationalism and the Soviet State 1953–1991* (Cambridge, MA, 1998).

15 Evgenii Chazov, *Zdorov'e i vlast': Vospominaniia 'Kremlevskogo vracha'* (Moscow, 1992), 80, 115, 127–8. Mark Kramer, 'The Czechoslovak Crisis and the Brezhnev Doctrine', in Carole Fink *et al.* (eds.), *1968: The World Transformed* (Washington and New York, 1998), 111–71; R. G. Pikhoia, 'Chekhoslovakiia, 1968 god. Vzgliad iz Moskvy po dokumentam TsK KPSS', *Novaia i noveishaia istoriia*, 6 (1994), 8–20; 1 (1995), 34–48.

16 Vladimir Kriuchkov, *Lichnoe delo* (Moscow, 1996), i. 97–8; Luba Brezhneva, *The World I Left Behind: Pieces of a Past* (New York, 1995), 363. See also Chazov, *Zdorov'e*, 139–48.

17 Stanislav Shatalin, '500 dnei i drugie dni moei zhizni', *Nezavisimaia gazeta*, 31 Mar. and 2 Apr. 1992; N. K. Baibakov, *Sorok let v pravitel'stve* (Moscow, 1993), 126–33.

18 Georgi Arbatov, *The System: An Insider's Life in Soviet Politics*

(New York, 1992), 259. On Andropov's high opinion of Gorbachev in 1977–8 as a 'convinced, consistent, and bold Communist' and 'a party organizer from the soil', see the testimony of a then-high-ranking KGB officer Viacheslav Kevorkov, *Tainyi kanal* (Moscow, 1997), 208–9. See also Chazov, *Zdorov'e*, 195.

19 Yegor Ligachev, *Inside Gorbachev's Kremlin* (New York, 1993), 24.

20 Leonov, *Likholet'e*, 136, 175. See also S. F. Akhromeev and G. M. Kornienko, *Glazami marshala i diplomata: Kriticheskii vzgliad na vneshniuiu politiku SSSR do i posle 1985 goda* (Moscow, 1992), 312.

21 Gorbachev, *Memoirs*, 164; Boldin, *Ten Years*, 60; Chazov, *Zdorov'e*, 212. The purported minutes of the politburo meetings, published in *Istochnik*, (1993), 0: 66–75, are an edited composite of the two sessions (10 Mar. and 11 Mar.).

22 On Tikhonov's ambitions, as relayed by KGB chief Chebrikov, see Gorbachev, *Memoirs*, 165; on Gromyko's ambitions, see the memoirs of Chebrikov's successor, Kriuchkov, *Lichnoe delo*, i. 253. Since the KGB provided security for all politburo members and for the entire communications network, Chebrikov was in a position to know the movements and no doubt the intentions of every major player.

23 *Izvestiia*, 2 Aug. 1984. Grishin writes in his memoirs, 'I think that in the KGB they kept a dossier on everyone of us, the members and candidate members of the politburo' (Viktor Grishin, *Ot Khrushcheva do Gorbacheva: Politicheskie portrety piati gensekov i A. N. Kosygina* (Moscow, 1996), 59).

24 Gorbachev, *Memoirs*, 164–6. See also Aleksandr Iakovlev, *OMUT pamiati* (Moscow, 2000), 442–3.

3. The drama of reform

1 Vladimir Medvedev, *Chelovek za spinoi* (Moscow, 1994), 208.

2 Agriculture was an even bigger conundrum. Subsidies for farming under Brezhnev totalled 19 billion roubles in 1977, or 70 roubles for every person in the country, but the Soviet Union still became dependent on millions of tons of grain imports from Canada and the US. Much of the harvest was left ungathered in the fields, and, even when collected, it often rotted in warehouses because of an extremely poor distribution network. Though a perpetual shambles, agriculture played a very prominent role in party careers. Peter Rutland, *The Politics of Economic Stagnation in the Soviet Union: The Role of Local Party Organs in Economic Management* (New York, 1993).

3 Boris Z. Rumer, *Soviet Steel: The Challenge of Industrial Modernization in the USSR* (Ithaca, NY, 1989).

4 Michael Ellman and Vladimir Kontorovich (eds.), *The Destruction of the Soviet Economic System: An Insiders' History* (Armonk, NY, 1998).

5 Precisely the same had transpired in Eastern Europe and, before that, in Latin America. During perestroika, it was instructive to have read a universal cautionary tale on the operation and effects of foreign 'aid': Graham Hancock, *Lords of Poverty: The Power, Prestige, and Corruption of the International Aid Business* (New York, 1989). On the chasm between 'aid' and direct foreign investment, see Brian Murray, 'Dollars and Sense: Foreign Investment in Russia and China', *Problems of Post-Communism*, 47/4 (2000), 24–33.

6 Ron McKay (ed.), *Letters to Gorbachev: Life in Russia through the Postbag of* Argumenty i fakty (London, 1991), 7–8, 161

(the letters were not written to Gorbachev). In the autumn of 1989, after the newspaper had published an unscientific 'poll' showing Gorbachev not to be the most popular politician in the country, he publicly ordered the editor, Vladislav Starkov, to resign; the country, Gorbachev exploded, was 'knee deep in gasoline' and journalists were throwing around matches. Starkov, a party member, defied the general secretary, and the matter was dropped.

7 Korotich and Cathy Porter, *The New Soviet Journalism: The Best of the Soviet Weekly Ogonyok* (Boston, 1990). Exaggeration of American economic and military capabilities had been characteristic of Soviet intelligence circles prior to 1985. The CIA (and especially the Pentagon) returned the 'favour', in spades.

8 Yegor Gaidar, *Days of Defeat and Victory* (Seattle, 1999), 31.

9 Iurii Shchekhochikhin, *Allo, my Vas slyshim: Iz khroniki nashego vremeni* (Moscow, 1987).

10 Ellen Mickiewicz, *Changing Channels: Television and the Struggle for Power in Russia* (New York, 1997), 69.

11 Gorbachev, *Memoirs*, 236.

12 *Sovetskaia Rossiia*, 13 Mar. 1988, translated in J. L. Black (ed.), *USSR Documents Annual 1988* (Gulf Breeze, FL, 1989), 275–81 (at 279).

13 Gorbachev, *Memoirs*, 252–3; Ligachev, *Inside*, 310. See also Vadim Medvedev, *V komande Gorbacheva: Vzgliad iznutri* (Moscow, 1994), 67–9; Anatolii Cherniaev, *Shest' let s Gorbachevym* (Moscow, 1993), 205–8; and Boldin, *Ten Years*, 168, who writes that Gorbachev at first viewed the Andreeva text as unexceptional. For a revealing look inside the CC apparat, which blames *it* for the Soviet collapse, see Leon Onikov, *KPSS: Anatomiia raspada* (Moscow, 1996).

14 Bill Keller, 'Conference Lifts Veil on Personalities and Intrigues', *New York Times*, 3 July 1988.

15 Beria also wanted to relinquish the millstone of East Germany, in exchange for a neutral, unified Germany. '"Novyi kurs" L.P. Berii', *Istoricheskii arkhiv*, 4 (1996), 132–63. See also Charles H. Fairbanks, Jr., 'National Cadres as a Force in the Soviet System: The Evidence of Beria's Career, 1949–1953', in Jeremy Azrael (ed.), *Soviet Nationality Policies and Practices* (New York, 1978), 144–86; and Mark Kramer, 'Declassified Materials from CPSU Central Committee Plenums: Sources, Context, Highlights', *Cahiers du Monde Russe*, 40/1–2 (1999), 271–306.

16 For Gorbachev as tactician, see Vitaly Tretyakov, 'Gorbachev's Enigma', *Moscow News*, 48 (1989).

17 Gorbachev, *Memoirs*, 293.

18 Akhromeev and Kornienko, *Glazami*, 312.

19 Ligachev, *Inside*, pp. xxxviii, 44. Ignorance was no excuse, he noted, since 'the politburo had virtually exhaustive information on all situations of conflict—political, economic, financial, interethnic' (p. 129). Nikolai Ryzhkov, Gorbachev's long-serving prime minister (1985–90), also condemned the 'betrayals' of perestroika. Ryzhkov, *Perestroika: Istoriia predatel'stv* (Moscow, 1992).

20 Boldin, acknowledging Yakovlev's importance, writes that the latter's relations with Gorbachev 'were not always smooth. Gorbachev always found ways of cramping Yakovlev's capacity for initiative' (Boldin, *Ten Years*, 160). Yakovlev writes that he and Gorbachev 'spoke almost everyday and rather frankly'. Iakovlev, *OMUT*, 444.

21 Leonid Shebarshin, chief of Soviet espionage who was sent to the three Baltic republics in the first half of 1990, found

'a huge staff of local KGB that did not know what they were working for, which issues they were to tackle, what information to collect and to whom they should report it' (Shebarshin, *Ruka Moskvy: Zapiski nachal'nika sovetskoi razvedki* (Moscow, 1992), 234).

22 He also apologized publicly for the civilian deaths, and launched an investigation that toyed with scapegoating the military, as had happened over the Georgian events of April 1989. Aleksandr Lebed', *Za derzhavu obidno . . .* (Moscow, 1995), 298–304.

4. Waiting for the end of the world

1 Leonov, *Likholet'e*, 192–212; Vojtech Mastny, 'The Soviet Non-Invasion of Poland in 1980/81 and the End of the Cold War', Cold War International History Project, working paper no. 23 (1998).

2 Gorbachev, *Memoirs*, 464–5. Ligachev concurred on the undesirability of using force to preserve Communism in Eastern Europe. David Remnick, *Lenin's Tomb: The Last Days of the Soviet Empire* (New York, 1993), 234. See also Jacques Lévesque, *The Enigma of 1989: The USSR and the Liberation of Eastern Europe* (Berkeley and Los Angeles, 1997).

3 Not only did Shevardnadze have no diplomatic training, but he had never even held a post in Moscow. Gorbachev's foreign ministry translator recalled the appointment of Shevardnadze as 'a real shocker' (Palazchenko, *My Years*, 30). Shevardnadze confessed that, 'even for the most kindly disposed, I was an outsider and a dilettante' (Shevardnadze, *The Future Belongs to Freedom* (New York, 1991), 42). On Shevardnadze's straightforwardness, see Anatoly Dobrynin, *In Confidence: Moscow's Ambassador to Six Cold War*

Presidents (New York, 1995), 575–6. Attitudes toward Shevardnadze in the US became extremely complimentary.

4 Philip Zelikow and Condoleezza Rice, *Germany United and Europe Transformed: A Study in Statecraft* (Cambridge, MA, 1995), 324–42.

5 Gorbachev, *Memoirs*, 516. In 1987 he had underscored the existence of two German states, adding, 'what there will be in a hundred years time is for history to decide' (Mikhail Gorbachev, *Perestroika: New Thinking for our Country and the World* (New York, 1987), 200).

6 Georgii Shakhnazarov, *Tsena svobody: Reformatsii Gorbacheva glazami ego pomoshchnika* (Moscow, 1994).

7 Angus Roxburgh, *The Second Russian Revolution: The Struggle for Power in the Kremlin* (London, 1991), 202.

8 Viktor Alksnis, *Sovetskaia Rossiia*, 21 Nov. 1990, as cited in Dmitrii Mikheyev, *The Rise and Fall of Gorbachev* (Indianapolis, IN, 1992), 113.

9 Leon Aron, *Yeltsin: A Revolutionary Life* (New York, 2000), 86. Although Yeltsin spent much of his two presidential terms in hospital or gloomy self-isolation, Aron compares him to Abraham Lincoln and Charles de Gaulle.

10 Boris Yeltsin, *Against the Grain: An Autobiography* (New York, 1990), 85–9.

11 Aleksandr Korzhakov, *Boris Yeltsin: Ot rassveta do zakata* (Moscow, 1997), 73–4. There is reason to credit Gorbachev's assertion that Yeltsin previously attempted suicide with a pair of scissors, just prior to the October 1987 party meeting that removed him as chief of the Moscow city party organization. Gorbachev, *Memoirs*, 246. See also Andrei Karaulov, *Plokhoi nachal'nik: Grustnaia kniga* (Moscow, 1996), 105; Aleksandr Kapto, *Na perekrestakh zhizhni: Politi-*

cheskie memuary (Moscow, 1996), 186. Gaidar is far more delicate about Yeltsin's depressions. Gaidar, *Days of Defeat*, 48.

12 Gorbachev, when he travelled the country, was held responsible for every aspect of daily life: people begged him for warm boots, fresh vegetables, school notebooks, an apartment, or a new kindergarten; everywhere it was something different, everywhere it was the same. See Medvedev, *Za spinoi cheloveka*, 206–22. When Yeltsin took to the road, he promised to deliver everything the people had expected of Gorbachev. Medvedev also notes that Raisa Gorbacheva would be seen on Soviet television during foreign trips changing outfits up to five times in a single day by people who could not find proper coats or shoes for their children or themselves. Yeltsin's wife, Naina, was rarely seen.

13 According to his press secretary, Gorbachev was ready to begin the signing with whichever republic agreed, as few as two. Andrei Grachev, *Kremlevskaia khronika* (Moscow, 1994), 176.

14 Boris Yelstin, *The Struggle for Russia* (New York, 1994), 38–9; Valentin Stepankov and Evgenii Lisov, *Kremlevskii zagovor* (Perm, 1993), 195; Kriuchkov, *Lichnoe delo*, ii. 132.

15 Kriuchkov, *Lichnoe delo*, i. 331–3. For a devastating portrait of the KGB chief, see Kalugin, *The First Directorate* (New York, 1994), 241–5. Nikolai Leonov, who did not suffer the ambitious Kalugin's disappointment at losing the post of KGB chief to Kriuchkov, paints a nuanced, but still damning portrait of the latter. Leonov, *Likholet'e*, 126–7, 235–7, 303–6. See also Shebarshin, *Ruka Moskvy*, 271, and Iakovlev, *Omut*, 237.

16 Another plotter, Valery Boldin, Gorbachev's chief of staff,

who preferred not to sign the Emergency Committee documents, re-entered the hospital during the putsch with a liver ailment. Stepankov and Lisov, *Kremlevskii zagovor*, 56–62, 85–101.

17 The Ukrainian leadership took no measures to assist Gorbachev, who was held on their territory (Crimea). Stuart Loory and Ann Imse, *Seven Days that Shook the World* (Atlanta, GA, 1991), 62–8.

18 *Komsomol'skaia Pravda*, 24 Aug. 1991; Evgenii Shaposhnikov, *Vybor*, 2nd edn. (Moscow, 1995), 39; Lebed', *Za derzhavu obidno*, 383–411; Yeltsin, *Struggle*, 92–3; Korzhakov, *Boris Yeltsin*, 93–5.

19 Gaidar, *Days of Defeat*, 62; Loory and Imse, *Seven Days*, 108.

20 Yevgenia Albats, *The State within a State: The KGB and its Hold on Russia—Past, Present, and Future* (New York, 1994), 191.

21 Leonov, *Likholet'e*, 383, 386. See also Shebarshin, *Ruka Moskvy*, 281; and Boldin, *Ten Years*, 30. Reflecting on the collapse, Leonov presented a constellation of causes but concluded that the 'one overarching factor' was 'lying. Lies struck at all aspects of our existence, becoming a fatal disease in our blood, destroying our soul' (p. 390).

22 Stepankov and Lisov, *Kremlevskii zagovor*, 209. Alexander Yakovlev recalled that Gorbachev dismissed his and others' warnings of a plot, reasoning that these men 'lacked the courage to stage a coup' (Radio Free Europe/Radio Liberty, *Daily Report*, 22 Aug. 1991, 3).

23 *Argumenty i fakty*, 38 (1991); *Literaturnaia gazeta*, 28 Aug. 1991.

24 Stepankov and Lisov, *Kremlevskii zagovor*, 102. Later, President Yeltsin would use the site of the plot (a new, well-equipped KGB recreational complex on Academician

Varga Street in south-west Moscow) to hold friendly meetings with the press. Viacheslav Kostikov, *Roman s prezidentom: Zapiski press-sekretaria* (Moscow, 1997), 78.

25 Yeltsin, *Struggle*, 70. On Yazov, see Lt. Gen. Leonid Ivashov, 'Marshall Yazov: Avgust 1991-go', *Krasnaia zvezda*, 21, 22, 25 Aug. 1992.

26 Dated 25 Aug. 1991, in Stepankov and Lisov, *Kremlevskii zagovor*, 258–9. Sergei Akhromeev, former chief of the General Staff and then the top military adviser to Gorbachev, committed suicide right after the failed putsch, leaving a note for the Soviet president: 'Beginning in 1990, I was convinced, as I am today, that our country is heading for ruin' (ibid. 214). The last KGB chief to have been arrested was Beria, who was executed in 1953. Kryuchkov would survive not only to write his memoirs and to enjoy retirement in freedom, but also to meet in 2000 with one of his successors as head of the KGB, Vladimir Putin, who by then had became Russia's President.

27 Viktor Baranets, *El'tsin i ego generaly: Zapiski polkovnika Genshtaba* (Moscow, 1997), 132–3.

28 On Gorbachev's unwillingness to relinquish his vision of reforming the party see Jack F. Matlock, Jr., *Autopsy on an Empire: The American Ambassador's Account of the Collapse of the Soviet Union* (New York, 1995), 596. See also Palazchenko, *My Years*, 142; and Iakovlev, *Omut*, 460–62.

29 Kryuchkov wrote: 'After every discussion of the situation in the country, Gorbachev as a rule gave instructions to continue the analysis and, just to be sure, to prepare recommendations. He did not exclude the possibility of enacting presidential or emergency rule in the country or in specific regions. All these materials were then returned for further

work, or with the command to "wait for the appropriate time"' (Kriuchkov, *Lichnoe delo*, ii. 146–7).

30 In mid-1990, the new prime minister of Russia's new government had gone on television to announce a telephone number for anyone interested in applying to become a minister. John Morrison, *Boris Yeltsin: From Bolshevik to Democrat* (New York, 1991), 154.

31 Roman Solchanyk, 'Ukraine', in Vera Tolz and Iain Elliot (eds.), *The Demise of the USSR: From Communism to Independence* (London, 1995), 119–29 (at 120).

32 Martha Brill Olcott, *Central Asia's New States: Independence, Foreign Policy, and Regional Security* (Washington, 1996), 9, 40. See also Nursultan Nazarbaev, *Bez pravykh i levykh* (Moscow, 1991), 178–81.

33 Jerry Hough, *Democratization and Revolution in the USSR 1985–1991* (Washington, 1997), 252.

34 Gorbachev, who writes that Yeltsin did not give up the idea of retaining some form of the Union until mid-October 1991, believed that he could get an agreement with Yeltsin one on one, but complains that Yeltsin would abandon it as soon as he returned to his entourage. Gorbachev, *Memoirs*, 347, 654; Grachev, *Kremlevskaia khronika*, 198–201.

35 David Remnick, *Resurrection: The Struggle for a New Russia* (New York, 1996), 27. The Russian official was evidently Andrei Kozyrev. Kozyrev, Gennadi Burbulis, and Sergei Shakhrai were the main CIS protagonists in the Yeltsin inner circle. Gaidar claims to have drafted the documents. Korzhakov, *Boris Yeltsin*, 129; Gaidar, *Days of Defeat*, 125.

36 Palazchenko, *My Years*, 347. 'Strategically, Gorbachev was completely oriented on Bush,' writes Kryuchkov. 'Attempts to caution him were met with a grin and objections. "Bush

won't let me down. Anyway, you can't trick me"'
(Kriuchkov, *Lichnoe delo*, ii. 45).

37 John Dunlop, *The Rise of Russia and the Fall of the Soviet Union*
(Princeton, 1993), 186–255; Amy Knight, *Spies without
Cloaks: The KGB's Successors* (Princeton, 1996), 12–37.

5. Survival and cannibalism in the rust belt

1 Steven L. Solnick, *Stealing the State: Control and Collapse in
Soviet Institutions* (Cambridge, MA, 1998), 6–7, 251.

2 Peter Reddaway and Dmitri Glinski, *The Tragedy of Russia's
Reforms: Market Bolshevism against Democracy* (Washington,
2001). One critic of shock therapy noted that, 'after six
years of Gorbachev's economic mismanagement, it was
probably too late, and conditions were too serious for
Yeltsin to attempt gradual reform' (Marshal Goldman, *Lost
Opportunity: What has Made Economic Reform in Russia so
Difficult* (New York, 1994), 156).

3 Hysteria over Russia's 'oligarchs' became widespread in the
US, but it contained no small element of hypocrisy.
Whereas, in 1999, executive pay was 13 times the average
worker's salary in Sweden, 15 times in Germany, and 24
times in the UK (the highest multiple in Europe), in the US
corporate executives took home 475 times more salary than
their average workers. Furthermore, American executives'
pay was increasing even though their companies' value was
declining. Here, perhaps, was the true meaning, for rank-
and-file shareholders, of corporate board 'oversight'.
'Executive Pay: A Special Report', *New York Times*, 1 Apr.
2001. See also Chrisopher Howard, *The Hidden Welfare
State: Tax Expenditures and Social Policy in the United States*
(Princeton, 1997).

4 Gaidar, *Days of Defeat*, 14–18, 79.

5 Soviet claims on Third World countries amounted to perhaps $150 billion, but in many cases these loans had been denominated in roubles, which after 1991 were undergoing steep devaluation. Also, many of the debtors were insolvent. Anders Aslund, *How Russia Became a Market Economy* (Washington, 1995), 105.

6 Kostikov, *Roman s prezidentom*, 42–3. Kostikov, Yeltsin's first-term press secretary, worked in the Kremlin office of the Stalin-era USSR President Mikhail Kalinin. Others who had used it included Voroshilov, Brezhnev, Podgorny, and, most immediately, Alexander Yakovlev (p. 37).

7 P. J. O'Rourke, 'Deep in the Heart of Siberia', *Rolling Stone*, 14 Nov. 1996, 95.

8 Vladimir Mau, *The Political History of Economic Reform in Russia, 1985–1994* (London, 1996), 72.

9 Gaidar, *Days of Defeat*, 203.

10 Boris Fedorov, *Desiat' bezumnykh let: Pochemu v Rossii ne sostoialis' reformy* (Moscow, 1999), 91–110.

11 David Woodruff, *Money Unmade: Barter and the Fate of Russian Capitalism* (Ithaca, NY, 1999), 99–102.

12 Jean Farneth Boone, 'Trading in Power: The Politics of Soviet Foreign Economic Relations, 1986–1991', Ph.D. dissertation, Georgetown University, 1998.

13 Gaidar, *Days of Defeat*, 97, 103.

14 Vladimir Shlapentokh, 'Russia: Privatization and Illegalization of Social and Political Life', *Washington Quarterly*, 19/1 (1996), 65–85 (at 73).

15 Remnick, *Resurrection*, 356.

16 Paul Klebnikov, *Godfather of the Kremlin: Boris Berezovsky and the Looting of Russia* (New York, 2000), 98.

17 Stephen Handleman, *Comrade Criminal: Russia's New Mafiya* (New Haven, 1995).

18 Anatolii Chubais (ed.), *Privatizatsiia po-rossiiski* (Moscow, 1999).

19 Chrystia Freeland, *Sale of the Century: Russia's Wild Ride from Communism to Capitalism* (New York, 2000), 67–8.

20 Joseph R. Blasi, Maya Kroumova, and Douglas Krause, *Kremlin Capitalism: Privatizing the Russian Economy* (Ithaca, NY, and London, 1997), 42. In Moscow, Mayor Yuri Luzhkov pulled strings in the Kremlin to exempt valuable city properties from the voucher scheme. Privatization of unique assets in the capital generated sizeable revenues, which were used not only to line the pockets of officials but also for infrastructure and services. Most accounts of privatization exclude Moscow, even though it is an immense part of the Russian economy.

21 David Hoffman, 'Russia's Clans Go to War', *Washington Post*, 26 Oct. 1997. Ironically, it was only after the 1997 sale of a quarter stake in Russia's telecom giant brought the first real privatization revenues to the state treasury that Chubais was dismissed from government, as a result of a scandal involving a book advance. (For the book, see n. 18.)

22 Maxim Boycko, Andrei Shleifer, and Robert Vishny, *Privatizing Russia* (Cambridge, MA, 1995), pp. vii, 97, 125.

23 Blasi *et al.*, *Kremlin Capitalism*, 170.

24 Gertrude Schroeder, 'Dimensions of Russia's Industrial Transformation, 1992 to 1998: An Overview', *Post-Soviet Geography and Economics*, 39/5 (1998), 243–70 (at 251).

25 Anders Aslund, 'Observations on the Development of Small Private Enterprises in Russia', *Post-Soviet Geography and Economics*, 38/4 (1997), 191–205.

26 Schroeder, 'Dimensions', 262.

27 Clifford Gaddy, *The Price of the Past: Russia's Struggle with the Legacy of a Militarized Economy* (Washington, 1996).

28 Woodruff, *Money Unmade*, 5; Andrei Shleifer and Daniel Treisman, *Without a Map: Political Tactics and Economic Reform in Russia* (Cambridge, MA, 2000), 73–7.

29 In Russian agriculture, the legacy of Soviet social welfare policies and entrenched social constituencies also shaped the possibilities and limits of rural 'reforms'. Stephen K. Wegren, *Agriculture and the State in Soviet and Post-Soviet Russia* (Pittsburgh, 1998).

30 Thane Gustafson, *Capitalism Russian-Style* (New York, 1999), 220.

31 Joseph Kahn and Timothy L. O'Brien, 'Easy Money: A Special Report. For Russia and its U.S. Bankers, Match Wasn't Made in Heaven', *New York Times*, 18 Oct. 1998; Murray, 'Dollars and Sense', 31. See also Thane Gustafson, *Capitalism Russian Style* (Cambridge, 1999).

32 George Soros, 'Who Lost Russia?', *New York Review of Books*, 13 Apr. 2000, 10–16. Bemoaning the stinginess of the West, one analyst noted that Russia's 'reform team faced a rather hopeless situation with the old bureaucracy' (Aslund, *How Russia Became*, 90). Another commentator urged the West to give $500 billion to Russia in 2000, after presenting copious evidence of official corruption. Stephen F. Cohen, *Failed Crusade: America and the Tragedy of Post-Communist Russia* (New York, 2000).

33 Richard E. Ericson, 'Economics and the Russian Transition', *Slavic Review*, 57/3 (1998), 609–25. The debate between shock therapists and gradualists, one scholar has

written, 'seems besides the point', because the evidence suggests that a country's proximity to the European Union border rather than its policy orientation shaped economic outcomes. Stephen E. Hanson, 'Analyzing Post-Communist Economic Change: A Review Essay', *East European Politics and Societies*, 12/1 (1998), 145–70.

6. Democracy without liberalism?

1 Eugene Huskey, *Presidential Power in Russia* (Armonk, NY, 1999), 13–16. Gorbachev's last prime minister, Valentin Pavlov, aptly called the presidential administration and CC apparat 'Siamese twins' (Pavlov, *Upushchen li shans?*, 167).

2 Because Yeltsin would not brook anyone who had worked too closely with Gorbachev, most of the top apparatchiks from the old CC ended up working for Khasbulatov, who had lost the Russian premiership to Gaidar, but whose team constantly outmanœuvred Gaidar and the Yeltsin entourage. Kostikov, *Roman*, 81. Khasbulatov, by the way, appropriated the apartment on Shchusev Street that had been built for Brezhnev but which Brezhnev (and later Yeltsin) declined to occupy as simply too large (460 square metres). Korzhakov, *Boris Yeltsin*, 138–46.

3 Thomas Graham, 'The Fate of the Russian State', *Demokratizatsiya*, 8/3 (2000), 354–75.

4 Korzhakov, the bodyguard, helped plan and led the assault on parliament, amid considerable wavering in the Defence Ministry and presidential staff. Korzhakov, *Boris Yeltsin*, 155–99 (quote p. 158).

5 Kostikov, *Roman*, 267.

6 It bears keeping in mind that, since the 1789 revolution,

France has had fifteen constitutions (and five different republics).

7   Eugene Huskey, 'The State–Legal Administration and the Politics of Redundancy', *Post-Soviet Affairs*, 11/2 (1995), 115–43. The Presidential Administration, like the old CC, came to control appointments to the ministries. At the same time, the Russian government, too, contained a large contingent of vice-premiers who did not have ministerial portfolios and whose trans-ministerial supervisory functions also recalled the overlord functions of the 'secretaries' of the old CC. Sergei Vasilyev, 'The Government of Russia', in Edward Skidelsky and Yuri Senokosov (eds.), *Russians on Russia* (London, 2000), 1–9.

8   Huskey, *Presidential Power*, 42.

9   Kostikov, *Roman*, 8; Korzhakov, *Boris Yeltsin*, 81–2; Boris Yeltsin, *Midnight Diaries* (New York, 2000), 112, 275. See also George Breslauer, 'Boris Yeltsin as Patriarch', *Post-Soviet Affairs*, 15/2 (1999), 186–200.

10 They were Chuvashiya, Tuva, and three republics in the North Caucasus, including Chechnya. Tuva, like Chechnya, bordered on another country (Mongolia), but was not violently separatist.

11 *Obshchaia gazeta*, 11–17 Dec. 1997. See also Anatol Lieven, *Chechnya: Tombstone of Russian Power* (New Haven, 1998).

12 Robert J. Kaiser, 'Prospects for the Disintegration of the Russian Federation', *Post-Soviet Geography*, 36/7 (1995), 426–35.

13 Mary McAuley, *Russia's Politics of Uncertainty* (New York, 1997), 222.

14 Valerii Streletskii, *Mrakobesie* (Moscow, 1998), 4; Korzhakov, *Boris Yeltsin*, 404.

15 Jeremy R. Azrael and Alexander G. Rahr, 'The Formation and Development of the Russian KGB, 1991–1994', RAND, Santa Monica, CA, 1993; Knight, *Spies without Cloaks*; Remnick, *Resurrection*, 186–95.

16 Gordon B. Smith, 'The Struggle over the Procuracy', in Peter H. Solomon (ed.), *Reforming Justice in Russia 1864–1996* (Armonk, NY, 1996), 348–73.

17 Todd Fogelsong, 'The Politics of Judicial Independence and the Administration of Criminal Justice in Soviet Russia, 1982–1992', Ph.D. dissertation, University of Toronto, 1995.

18 Peter H. Solomon, 'The Limits of Legal Order in Post-Soviet Russia', *Post-Soviet Affairs*, 11/2 (1995), 89–114.

19 Kathryn Hendley, 'Rewriting the Rules of the Game in Russia: The Neglected Issue of the Demand for Law', *East European Constitutional Review*, 8/4 (1999), 89–95.

20 Tim McDaniel, *The Agony of the Russian Idea* (Princeton, 1996). The author universalizes the agony of the now impoverished intelligentsia. Eternally apocalyptic, the intelligentisa finally lived to see the day it helped topple a system that had provided immense subsidies for culture and shielded it from the exigencies of the mass market.

7. Idealism and treason

1 See the candid, incisive testimony by the Reagan and Bush envoy to Moscow, Matlock, *Autopsy on an Empire*. Reagan came around much more quickly than did Bush.

2 Daniel Patrick Moynihan, *Secrecy: The American Experience* (New Haven, 1998).

3 Rather than Reagan's earlier posture of confrontation, it was his later policy ('Reagan II') of deep détente that

proved important, since it allowed Gorbachev considerable room unintentionally to destroy the system. But that, of course, had not been the aim behind Reagan's policy reversal. His administration belatedly embraced Gorbachev because of the latter's offer of asymmetrical Soviet cuts in arms control deals, made without holding to demands that the US relinquish its cherished, chimerical pursuit of Star Wars. On Reagan, see Gary Wills, *Reagan's America: Innocents at Home* (Garden City, NY, 1987), 358; Edward Tabor Linenthal, *Symbolic Defense: The Cultural Significance of the Strategic Defense Initiative* (Urbana, IL, 1989), 9; and Frances Fitzgerald, *Way Out There in the Blue: Reagan, Star Wars, and the End of the Cold War* (New York, 2000).

4 John Morrison (ed.), *Mikhail Gorbachev, an Intimate Biography* (New York, 1988), 59–60; Zdeněk Mlynář, 'Il mio compagno di studi Mikhail Gorbachiov', *L'Unità*, 9 Apr. 1985; Gorbachev, *Memoirs*, 81–2.

5 Vladimir Bukovsky, 'Who Resists Gorbachev?', *Washington Quarterly*, 12/1 (1989), 5–19.

6 For the disorientation, in practical policy terms that resulted, see Cherniaev, *Shest' let*, 279–80.

7 Medvedev, *V komande Gorbacheva*, 76–7, 93–7.

8 During perestroika, Gorbachev painstakingly rewrote his long speeches to incorporate more Marxist-Leninist theory than even his apparatchik speech-writers included. He was the only General Secretary to make a pilgrimage to the place of Lenin's Siberian exile. He also read Lenin constantly, particularly in the years up to 1989. Such actions were meant to put Gorbachev on Lenin's level. They were also heartfelt. Boldin, *Ten Years*, 95; Volkogonov, *Autopsy for an Empire*, 443. 'The paradox of Gorbachev', wrote

Volkogonov, 'can be simply expressed: the man who killed Communism was a convinced Communist' (p. 474).

9 Having begun as a party-sanctioned, peasant-led de-collectivization of agriculture, the Chinese reforms evolved into a combination of abundant cheap labour from rural hinterlands, foreign capital funnelled partly through Hong Kong's long-standing capitalist institutions and nearly unrestricted export access to the gigantic US consumer market (open access to which had also been a source of the Japanese and then South Korean 'miracles'). As of 2001, China was continuing to press forward with capitalist institution building, but it had unstable mechanisms of political succession, and was also threatened over the medium term by far-reaching resource shortages and looming ecological catastrophe.

10 The only major open KGB insubordination took place in January 1991, in Boris Yeltsin's home town of Sverdlovsk (Yekaterinburg), when officers refused to carry out what they regarded as their bosses' retrograde orders, but within four months all sixty-four protesters had been fired. *Komsomol'skaia Pravda*, 8 May 1991; Shebarshin, *Ruka Moskvy*, 269.

11 Vadim Bakatin, USSR interior minister, had been officially transferring ministry personnel and property to republic jurisdiction before being replaced in late 1990. Valentin Pavlov, *Avgust iznutri* (Moscow, 1993), 31; Kriuchkov, *Lichnoe delo*, i. 437.

12 William E. Odom, *The Collapse of the Soviet Military* (New Haven, 1998), 297–8.

13 Matlock, *Autopsy*, 599, 656–3.

14 One scholar has written that, 'historically, none of the

overextended, multinational empires ever retreated to their own ethnic base until they had been defeated in a Great Power war'. In 1991, one did. Paul Kennedy, *The Rise and Fall of the Great Powers: Economic Change and Military Conflict from 1500 to 2000* (New York, 1987), 514.

15 By 1998, the money loaned to Russia's government (as 'aid'), was being earmarked solely to pay back previous IMF loans. Despite receiving approximately $60 billion in loans during the 1990s (which compounded the inherited Soviet debt burden), Russia's succession of administrations implemented few of the Western prescriptions that were supposedly hard-and-fast preconditions to qualify for the 'aid'.

16 Murray Feshbach and Alfred Friendly, Jr., *Ecocide in the USSR: Health and Nature under Siege* (New York, 1992), 1.

17 *Nuclear Successor States of the Soviet Union: Status Report on Nuclear Weapons, Fissile Material, and Export Controls* (Monterey Institute of International Studies–Carnegie Endowment for International Peace, Mar. 1998). As of the end of 2000, one American journalist reported, the US Department of Defense 'Cooperative Threat Reduction' programmes had helped deactivate 5,288 Russian missile warheads, destroy 419 long-range nuclear missiles and 367 silos, eliminate 81 bombers, 292 submarine missile launchers and 174 submarine missiles, and seal 194 nuclear test holes and sites in Russia and other former Soviet republics. Judith Miller, 'U.S. Reviewing Aid Meant to Contain Russia's Arsenal', *New York Times*, 29 Mar. 2001. Russia still had at least 6,000 operational long-range nuclear weapons, in addition to bomb-grade fuel for making tens of thousands more.

18 *Eliminating a Deadly Legacy of the Cold War: Overcoming Obs-tacles to Russian Chemical Disarmament* (Monterey–Moscow Study Group on Russian Chemical Disarmament, Jan. 1998). Even if secured from theft or rogue sale, Russia's chemical weapons, stored at seven known sites, posed enormous health risks. David Hoffman, 'Chemical Dumps Expose Russia to Big Health Risks', *Washington Post*, 16 Aug. 1998. The US inventory of 32,000 tons of chemical weapons was being destroyed at an estimated cost of $13 billion.

19 Ken Alibek with Stephen Handelman, *Biohazard* (New York, 1999).

20 Matthew Bunn, Oleg Bukharin, Jill Cetina, Kenneth Luongo, and Frank von Hippel, 'Retooling Russia's Nuclear Cities', *Bulletin of the Atomic Scientists*, 54/5 (1998), 44–50.

21 John B. Dunlop, *The Faces of Contemporary Russian National-ism* (Princeton, 1983), p. ix. Dunlop advised US policy-makers to add Russia to the list of 'captive nations' within the Soviet Union (pp. 286–7), anticipating Boris Yeltsin's Union-busting campaign.

22 None of the three countries admitted to NATO in the 1990s (Poland, Czech Republic, Hungary) completed sup-posedly mandatory military reforms before their admission. Nor did they do so afterwards. But, unlike NATO, the EU would not allow membership without transformation of institutions, from courts and the corpus of laws to account-ing practices and financial systems. It remained to be seen whether the above leading accession countries would manage to meet EU requirements, or whether their EU admission would be further postponed.

23 See William Thomas Stead, *The Americanization of the World, or, The Trend of the Twentieth Century* (New York, H. Markley, [1902]), who expressed anxiety about the future of the mighty British Empire, and, on the basis of 'racial' affinity, advocated 'merging' with the US; otherwise, he warned that Britain would be faced with 'our suppression by the United States as the centre of gravity in the English-speaking world . . . and the ultimate reduction to the status of an English-speaking Belgium' (p. 396).

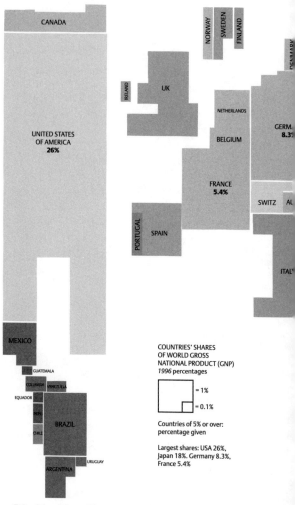

COUNTRIES' SHARES
OF WORLD GROSS
NATIONAL PRODUCT (GNP)
1996 percentages

☐ = 1%
☐ = 0.1%

Countries of 5% or over:
percentage given

Largest shares: USA 26%,
Japan 18%. Germany 8.3%,
France 5.4%

3 World national income statistics

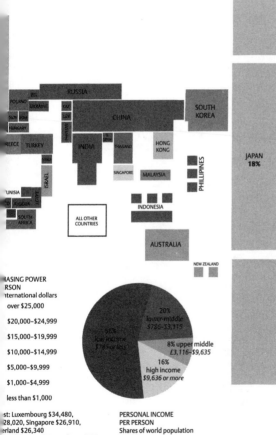

RUSSIA
POLAND BEL UKRAINE XXX
SVK LOX
HUNGARY
GREECE TURKEY
ISRAEL
TUNISIA
ALGERIA EGYPT
SOUTH AFRICA
ALL OTHER COUNTRIES
CHINA
INDIA
THAILAND
SINGAPORE MALAYSIA
INDONESIA
HONG KONG
SOUTH KOREA
PHILLIPINES
JAPAN 18%
AUSTRALIA
NEW ZEALAND

...ASING POWER
RSON
...ternational dollars

over $25,000
$20,000–$24,999
$15,000–$19,999
$10,000–$14,999
$5,000–$9,999
$1,000–$4,999
less than $1,000

56% low income $785 or less
20% lower-middle $786–$3,115
8% upper middle $3,116–$9,635
16% high income $9,636 or more

...st: Luxembourg $34,480,
...28,020, Singapore $26,910,
...erland $26,340
...st: Ethiopia and Mozambique $500,
...Leone $510, Burundi $590

...e; *World Bank Atlas 1998*

PERSONAL INCOME
PER PERSON
Shares of world population
in each income group
1996 percentages

Source: *World Bank Atlas 1998*

♦ Chemical weapons storage facilities
★ Biological weapons production, R&D, and test sites
⊕ Nuclear missiles, bombers, submarines, and launchers, nuclear facilities,
   and secret cities

4 Russia's doomsday complex

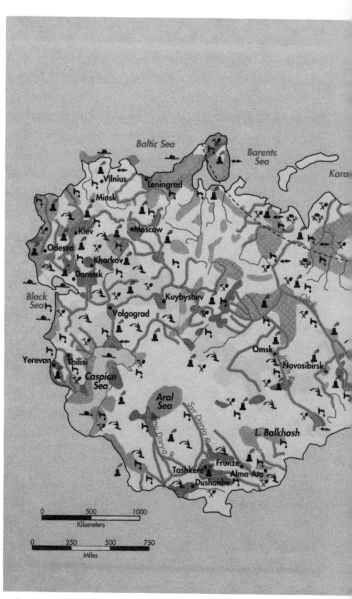

5 Soviet and post-Soviet ecocide

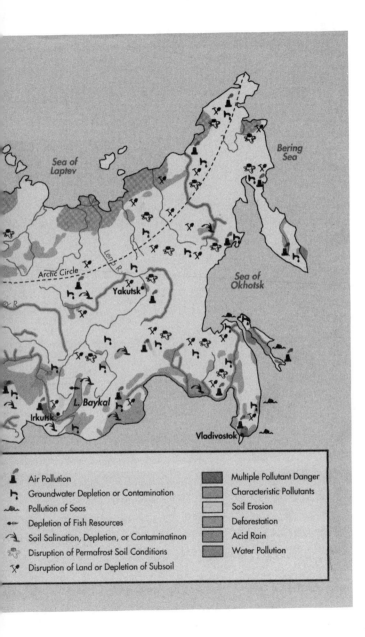

Sea of
Laptev

Bering
Sea

Arctic Circle

Lena R.

ey R.

Yakutsk

Sea of
Okhotsk

L. Baykal

Irkutsk

Vladivostok

Air Pollution

Groundwater Depletion or Contamination

Pollution of Seas

Depletion of Fish Resources

Soil Salination, Depletion, or Contaminatinon

Disruption of Permafrost Soil Conditions

Disruption of Land or Depletion of Subsoil

Multiple Pollutant Danger

Characteristic Pollutants

Soil Erosion

Deforestation

Acid Rain

Water Pollution

Further reading

Probably the best starting point for analyses of the Soviet collapse is Fred Halliday, 'A Singular Collapse: The Soviet Union, Market Pressure and Inter-State Competition', *Contention*, 1/2 (1992), 121–41. Another concise, early overview of explanatory factors can be found in Alexander Dallin, 'Causes of the Collapse of the USSR', *Post-Soviet Affairs*, 8/2 (1992), 279–302. Unusually suggestive essays include Vladimir Bukovsky, 'Who Resists Gorbachev?', *Washington Quarterly*, 12/1 (1989), 5–19; 'Djilas on Gorbachev', *Encounter*, 71/3 (1988), 3–19; Donna Bahry, 'Society Transformed? Rethinking the Social Roots of Perestroika', *Slavic Review*, 52/3 (1993), 512–54; and Alex Alexiev, 'Soviet Nationalities in German Wartime Strategy 1941–1945', RAND, Santa Monica, CA, 1982. For the post-mortems among Sovietologists, there is Michael Cox (ed.), *Rethinking the Soviet Collapse: Sovietology, the Death of Communism and the New Russia* (London, 1998).

Unfortunately, most of the avalanche of Soviet and post-Soviet memoirs have not been translated into English, including exceptionally valuable ones by bodyguards, press secretaries, prime ministers, officers of the general staff and army command, high officials of the KGB, and the long-serving Kremlin doctor. Valuable secondary studies on the collapse are Steven L. Solnick, *Stealing the State: Control and Collapse in Soviet Institutions* (Cambridge, MA, 1998); John Dunlop, *The Rise of Russia and the Fall of the Soviet Empire* (Princeton, 1993, 1995); Murray

Feshbach and Alfred Friendly, Jr., *Ecocide in the USSR* (London, 1992); Kazimierz Z. Poznański, *Poland's Protracted Transition: Institutional Change and Economic Growth 1970–1994* (New York, 1996); and Charles S. Maier, *Dissolution: The Crisis of Communism and the End of East Germany* (Princeton, 1997). Alternatives to the interpretation presented here can be found in Moshe Lewin, *The Gorbachev Phenomenon* (Berkeley and Los Angeles, 1988, 1991); Scott Shane, *Dismantling Utopia: How Information Ended the Soviet Union* (Chicago, 1994); Ben Fowkes, *The Disintegration of the Soviet Union: A Study in the Rise and Triumph of Nationalism* (New York, 1997); and Robert M. Gates, *From the Shadows: The Ultimate Insider's Story of Five Presidents and How They Won the Cold War* (New York, 1996). Valerie Bunce, *Subversive Institutions: The Design and Destruction of Socialism and the State* (New York, 1999), also argues that Soviet institutions subverted themselves, but her explanation differs from that offered here.

Few books on post-Soviet Russia take account of the Soviet collapse or exhibit a grasp of history, geopolitics, and institutions. Exceptions include Eugene Huskey, *Presidential Power in Russia* (Armonk, NY, 1999); Mary McAuley, *Russia's Politics of Uncertainty* (New York, 1997); Clifford G. Gaddy, *The Price of the Past: Russia's Struggle with the Legacy of a Militarized Economy* (Washington, 1996); William E. Odom, *The Collapse of the Soviet Military* (New Haven, 1998); and David Woodruff, *Money Unmade: Barter and the Fate of Russian Capitalism* (Ithaca, NY, 1999). Among outstanding short pieces are Thomas Graham, 'The Fate of the Russian State', *Demokratizatsiya*, 8/3 (2000), 354–75; Richard E. Ericson, 'Economics and the Russian Transition', *Slavic Review*, 57/3 (1998), 609–25; Vladimir Shlapentokh, 'Russia: Privatization and Illegalization of Social and Political Life', *Washington Quarterly*, 19/1 (1996), 65–85; Jeremy

R. Azrael and Alexander G. Rahr, 'The Formation and Development of the Russian KGB, 1991–1994', RAND, Santa Monica, CA, 1993; and Peter H. Solomon, 'The Limits of Legal Order in Post-Soviet Russia', *Post-Soviet Affairs*, 11/2 (1995), 89–114. Analyses of Russia that differ from that expressed here can be found in Tim McDaniel, *The Agony of the Russian Idea* (Princeton, 1996), and Peter Reddaway and Dmitri Glinski, *The Tragedy of Russia's Reforms: Market Bolshevism Against Democracy* (Washington, 2001).

Typically, English-language journalism on the late Soviet Union and especially post-Soviet Russia left something to be desired, but numerous instances of outstanding reporting are cited in the notes. Very highly recommended is Ryszard Kapuściński, *Imperium* (New York, 1994).

Perhaps the most incisive, albeit brief, discussion of the wider significance of Russia's example can be found in Stephen Holmes, 'What Russia Teaches us Now: How Weak States Threaten Freedom', *American Prospect*, 33 (1997), 30–9.

For those interested in studying the art of contemporary history, there is no better place to turn than Thucydides, *The Peloponnesian War* (New York, 1951).

Index